Micro Radio and the FCC

Micro Radio and the FCC

*Media Activism and the Struggle
over Broadcast Policy*

Andy Opel

Westport, Connecticut
London

Library of Congress Cataloging-in-Publication Data

Opel, Andrew, 1964–
  Micro radio and the FCC : media activism and the struggle over broadcast policy /
Andy Opel.
    p. cm.
  Includes bibliographical references and index.
  ISBN 0–275–97914–8 (alk. paper)
    1. Pirate radio broadcasting—United States. 2. Low power radio—United States. 3. Radio
broadcasting policy—United States. I. Title.
  HE8697.65.U6O63 2004
  384.54′0973—dc22   2003062441

British Library Cataloguing in Publication Data is available.

Library of Congress Catalog Card Number: 2003062441
ISBN: 0–275–97914–8

First published in 2004

Praeger Publishers, 88 Post Road West, Westport, CT 06881
An imprint of Greenwood Publishing Group, Inc.
www.praeger.com

Printed in the United States of America

The paper used in this book complies with the
Permanent Paper Standard issued by the National
Information Standards Organization (Z39.48–1984).

10 9 8 7 6 5 4 3 2 1

To my father, who taught me to speak truth to power.

Contents

Acknowledgments

This book was made possible with the help of an amazing group of supportive people. I would like to thank Jane Brown for her guidance and counsel throughout my stay at University of North Carolina. I could not have done this without her encouragement and support. I would also like to thank Lucila Vargas for encouraging me to research alternative media, Don Shaw for showing me how to remain a free thinker over a long career, Larry Grossberg for helping me connect critical cultural theory and everyday politics, and Dorothy Holland for modeling academic activism. In addition, Jay Hamilton and Ted Coopman gave me invaluable feedback and helped me revise this manuscript and Bob McChesney has been very generous with his time and energy. Jeff Goodman also provided me excellent feedback on my ideas and writing throughout the development of this book.

I would also like to thank Ansje for all her love and support and Buster for reminding me to exercise. Also, I would like to thank the community of people in Carrboro, North Carolina, the friends in Tallahassee, Florida, and the wide circle of academic and activists that work so hard to make this world a better place.

Introduction: Watching a Media Movement Work

Driving across the United States, it is easy to surf the radio dial and ride a wave of "classic rock" from New York to Los Angeles. From syndicated talk radio to standardized music formats, the airwaves increasingly reflect the consolidation and mergers that have swept through the media industry at the turn of the millennium. Even public radio stations are increasingly dominated by nationally distributed productions such as "All Things Considered," "A Prairie Home Companion," and "Car Talk." This homogenization of radio and resulting lack of localism has inspired a wide range of people to take to the airwaves in hopes of restoring some of the voices and perspectives lost in an increasingly franchised marketplace of ideas. These activists have combined a material practice of direct-action illegal radio broadcasting often called pirate radio or more recently "micro radio," with a discursive practice of articulating principles of democracy, diversity, and media access.

This book is an attempt to understand how media activists have challenged current broadcast policy and how the government and the larger commercial and noncommercial broadcasting industry have responded to those challenges. Why did this challenge to broadcast policy arise in the late 1990s? What were the conditions of possibility that helped to shape and define micro radio? How is micro radio activism similar and different from other social movements such as the environmental, women's rights, or civil rights movements? This book approaches these questions by tracing the discourse generated by the micro radio activists as it moved from discussions within the movement, through the media, and eventually into Federal Communications Commission (FCC) policy.

This book is a close examination of the struggle over micro radio. Throughout this research micro radio is viewed as a site of social activity, a unique cultural and historical nexus where ideas about the relationship between media and democracy are explored. This research makes the case that the struggle over micro radio is the most recent manifestation of a growing social movement, a movement of media reform. Like the environmental movement that emerged during the 1960s and 1970s and coalesced around specific issues, such as nuclear power or the extinction of the whales, the media activism and reform movement (MARM) discovered a significant formative issue in micro radio at the turn of the millennium.

As grassroots activists, policy think tanks, and academic scholars explored the issues and possibilities raised by micro radio, ideas and practices that had been below the surface of widespread consciousness began to reach a public audience. Concerns about the effects of concentrated ownership of media technology, the prevalence of commercial media, and the lack of public access to local media outlets (radio and TV in particular) have gained increasing attention as our information-based society and economy has come into bloom at the start of the twenty-first century. Thus the struggle over micro radio did not appear out of the blue, stumbled upon by radio hobbyists. Rather, it is connected to a long history of media reform struggles throughout the twentieth century including the debates over (non)commercial radio in the 1920s and 1930s (McChesney, 1993), through the debates over the fairness doctrine and more recently cable television regulation.

The issues raised by micro radio have been studied and researched for many years from many theoretical and methodological perspectives. Concerns about the consolidation of media ownership, radio and television content, notions of the public interest, localism, and public access to media technology have all been problematized by a host of scholars and activists, albeit in a fragmented and often publicly invisible way. Micro radio provided an accessible, affordable technology with which to demonstrate the power and potential of local, alternative-community media-making. And with that media making came a host of regulatory issues as micro radio enthusiasts quickly discovered how limited access to the publicly owned electromagnetic spectrum was.

Micro radio became a lightning rod for the emerging media activism and reform movement. As local people took to the airwaves, illegally broadcasting everything from the frivolous to the serious, theoretical concepts such as localism and public access suddenly became grounded in a real world radio show. Micro radio broadcasters were able to demonstrate what is *not* included in most mainstream media and in the process, show what can happen when a diverse public is allowed to access the most ubiquitous telecommunications technology of the day. Continuing the environmental analogy, species protection needed to be demonstrated before the concept of ecology could be integrated into the fabric of social life. Thirty-five years after Rachel Carson's book, *Silent Spring*, we now assume a potential threat from pesticides. In addition, curbside recycling is common across the country, as are efficiency ratings on appliances. Though the goals of many environmentalists are far from being achieved and the project of the environmental movement is far from complete, many of the movement's concepts about humans' relationship to nature have been integrated into popular practices and conceptions of life. Thus, the environmental movement explored the realms of ecology and in the process created whole new sets of knowledge and practices about our relationship to the environment. This social movement also created a worldview, cosmology if you will, that connected the actions of people to the other natural processes of the planet.

This book argues that a similar process of reconceptualization of the media is taking place in the United States at the turn of the millennium. Like the environmental movement, the media activism and reform movement is raising questions about the role of media in social life, questioning the organization of the media, and working to reestablish the power and potential of local people communicating with one another without the intervention of a multinational global media corporation. These issues were explored extensively through the struggle to license low-power, micro radio. This site of struggle allowed the many diverse contributors to this movement; grassroots pirate broadcasters, media policy professionals, and academic scholars, to join forces and articulate the issues and demonstrate alternatives to the dominant media. These issues were articulated through a discourse that focused on diversity, the public interest, localism, noncommercialism, and civil rights. They were enacted and presented to government officials at the FCC as well as broader audiences through the mass media. Thus the knowledge and practices of the media activism and reform movement were distributed and made visible via the micro radio issue, demonstrated on the radio dial, and integrated into a growing re-cognition of the interconnections between media and society.

This book outlines the contours of the emerging media activism and reform movement. Social movement theories offer a range of definitions for determining when special issue advocacy achieves the status of a "social movement." This book draws on new social movement theory and the work of Eyerman and Jamison (1991) to examine the various efforts to promote micro radio in particular and issues of media and democracy in general. Although a wide range of activity by a host of groups and individuals is taking place across the United States, widespread conceptions of "media activism" have yet to be integrated into public awareness. Whereas the environmental movement received large-scale, popular attention through work such as Carson's *Silent Spring,* media activism has yet to experience such a cultural wake-up call. Thus the media activism and reform movement may in fact be a "proto social movement," a movement in need of a larger cultural watershed than micro radio that moves concerns about media and democracy from the special interests of activists and academics to a broader public audience of concerned citizens. This question of the status of the media activism and reform movement is explored throughout this book.

BACKGROUND AND CONTEXT

In 1978, the FCC stopped issuing Class D radio broadcast licenses, requiring all new stations to meet the Class C requirements and broadcast at a minimum power of 100 watts. The new ruling forced existing Class D license holders to change frequency and/or location if they interfered with "full-power" broadcast stations. Up until this time, the Class D permits were issued to noncommercial, educational organizations, allowing them to operate small (less than 100 watts) radio stations.

The 1978 ruling, combined with a number of other factors, set in motion a series of events that has led to the present micro radio movement in the United States.

Since the Communications Act of 1934 became law, there have been unlicensed radio broadcasters. Called pirate radio and more recently micro radio broadcasters, these illegal broadcasters have received a fair amount of attention from the press and the FCC in the past few years. In 1998 for example, the FCC reported shutting down more then 250 unlicensed micro broadcasters (Kennard, 1998b), and the popular press estimated that up to 1,000 other illegal micro stations continued to operate in the continental United States at the time (Hornblower, 1998). Micro broadcasters used small, low-cost transmitters (usually between 10 and 40 watts) to start radio stations designed to serve very local populations, filling the void created by the elimination of the Class D licenses. Depending on the geographic terrain, these signals covered an area with a radius of one to ten miles. Stations have appeared from the Lower East Side of Manhattan to the wheat fields of North Dakota. The content ranges from Christian talk radio to round-the-clock local music, from Portuguese community affairs to coverage of local town meetings (Ferguson, 1998). These stations claimed to offer something unique and vital to their listening areas. By going on the air in violation of the law, micro radio broadcasters confronted the policies of the FCC and attempted to expand the marketplace of ideas to include the corner store as well as the corporate supermarket chain. What these disparate stations had in common was their outlaw status and their civil disobedience.

SIGNIFICANCE

On January 29, 1999, the FCC issued a "Notice of Proposed Rulemaking" for the creation of a low-power (1–1,000 watt) radio. Appearing after a year of high-profile micro station shutdowns and arrests by the FCC and many years of legal disputes in the courts (Coopman, 1998), these proposed rules reversed two decades of FCC policy and enforcement. The FCC notice that outlined the proposal to license low-power FM (LPFM) stations left many important questions unanswered. Would low-power stations be commercial or noncommercial, open to multiple ownership by individuals or a corporation, and to whom would they be available? How large a transmitter could be used? These questions were left unanswered in the initial proposal by the FCC precipitated a wide range of responses from various interests groups during the ensuing public comment period.

The micro radio activists, in cooperation with the National Lawyers Guild, the Media Access Project, and many other groups and individuals, proposed a series of guidelines to protect the new low-power stations from becoming small versions of the predominant commercial radio landscape. The guidelines, put together by the micro radio empowerment coalition, encouraged the FCC to protect the distinction between low-power radio and the predominant commercial and noncommercial radio. These guidelines included ownership limits of one station per owner with the owner living within the broadcast area of the station, noncommercial status for all low-power stations, and amnesty for all illegal broadcasters.

After several extensions of the public comment period initiated by the National Association of Broadcasters (NAB), the FCC closed the public comment period in October 1999. On January 27, 2000, almost one year after the proposed rule making, the FCC adopted new rules creating the LPFM radio service. In these new rules, the FCC followed the guidelines articulated by the micro radio empowerment coalition, granting universal noncommercial status, a one-station ownership limit, and a limited amnesty for illegal broadcasters.

The micro radio activists' proposal was in direct opposition to the desires of the broadcast industry as represented by the NAB. The NAB opposed the entire low-power radio initiative and was especially dissatisfied with the LPFM service proposed by the FCC. This dissatisfaction resulted in an attempt to reverse the FCC's decision through congressional action. The U.S. House of Representatives passed HR 3439, The Radio Broadcasting Preservation Act of 2000, April 13, 2000. This bill revoked the amnesty offered to illegal broadcasters and increased the spacing between radio stations, greatly reducing the number of possible spaces in which low-power stations could operate. The Senate drafted similar legislation (S 3020) in the fall of 2000. Because of President Clinton's threaten to veto this legislation, a stand-alone version of the radio preservation act was never submitted to the president. Instead, the text of the act was added to an appropriations bill as a rider and President Clinton signed this bill into law on December 23, 2000.

This series of events poses interesting questions for communications policy research. How was a grassroots movement able to affect national policy during a period of unprecedented consolidation in a promarket, neoliberal economic context? How did a public agency move from defender of the status quo to an advocate of change? What are some of the possible implications of this decision on such policy concepts as "public interest" and "localism"? This exceptional case serves as a starting point in finding answers to these questions.

CORE PROPOSITION AND KEY CONCEPTS

This examination of broadcast policy change in the United States is rooted in the core proposition that the decision to license LPFM was an anomaly in the dominant trend of broadcast regulation. LPFM presented the opportunity for small-scale, local individuals and grassroots organizations to access the most ubiquitous communications technology available. In the face of decreased regulation, the easing of public interest standards and requirements for broadcasters, and large-scale consolidation across the media landscape, this policy created a new opportunity for community media. Given the unique features of LPFM policy, the emergence of vigorous grassroots, social movement activism around the issues of broadcast policy becomes an interesting area of inquiry for communication scholars and practitioners alike.

Imbedded with the core proposition that LPFM policy was anomalous in the context of larger broadcast regulation trends are sets of key concepts that have been explored in previous literature. These key concepts fall into three sets of ideas beginning with the history of low-power and community radio. The second set of ideas includes the importance of community media in relation to the concepts of localism, militant particularism, and the public interest. The relationship between community media and the political and economic restructuring associated with globalization was especially significant to this area. The third area of key concepts involves micro radio as a site of media activism. Micro radio activism will be put in the context of social movement theory and located as a site where the emerging media activism and reform movement temporarily coalesced and gained broad-based public visibility.

A BRIEF HISTORY OF LOW-POWER
COMMUNITY RADIO

From the earliest attempts, government regulation of radio broadcasting has been a contentious issue. Lawrence Soley (1999), author of *Free Radio: Electronic Civil Disobedience*, outlined the rise and fall of low power radio from the end of World War II through 1998. Although FM radio was invented in the 1930s, after the war the FCC changed the frequencies dedicated to FM, thus making many of the receivers available at the time obsolete. The new frequencies, 88–108 MHz, are what we use today. As a way to appease critics of the frequency change, "the FCC reserved frequencies between 88 and 92 MHz for educational, noncommercial broadcasting" (Soley, 1999, p. 39). Because few radios at the time could receive these frequencies, they had little commercial value. Universities and nonprofit groups supported the frequency change and ensuing bandwidth designation in spite of the limited audience potential. To encourage these groups who lacked the funding for large-scale stations, in 1948 the FCC allowed low-power (10-watt) noncommercial broadcasting on those frequencies (Soley, 1999).

Although the number of low-power stations increased through the 1950s and early 1960s, Soley argues that it was not until the late 1960s that low-power community radio began to blossom. Soley describes three types of noncommercial radio stations occupying this bandwidth by the late 1960s: (1) college radio stations, (2) nonlocal community radio, and (3) local community radio. College and university stations provided a hands-on learning environment and outlet for students. As a parenthetical note, I was a DJ on my high school radio station, WHSR (Winchester High School Radio) three hours a week for all four years of high school. WHSR was a 10-watt station that has since been forced off the air.

Nonlocal community radio is exemplified by Pacifica stations such as KPFA in Berkeley, California. Started in 1949, KPFA and the Pacifica network have encountered periodic conflicts because of oversight by a national advisory board. Although advised by (local) community members, Pacifica stations are not owned or controlled by the community (Soley, 1999). Tension between the national advisory board and local Pacifica station staff has erupted throughout the history of Pacifica radio. Most recently, in a move to increase market share by appealing to a broader audience, the Pacifica board fired a number of people from the flagship station KPFA and initiated a midnight lockout and staff reorganization at WBAI in New York City on Christmas Eve 2000. The National Pacifica Board was involved in an ongoing struggle with Amy Goodman, the host of "Democracy Now," over who will determine the talk show's topics (FAIR, 2000).

An example of the third type of community radio station described by Soley is KRAB, a locally owned and operated community radio station in Seattle. Founded by Lorenzo Milam in 1964 in response to the Pacifica model, KRAB was owned and managed locally. This model was replicated in a number of cities nationwide, where a few stations continue to operate in the local community tradition.

Amid the rise of low-power, noncommercial radio, the FCC passed the Public Broadcasting Act of 1967, which established the Corporation for Public Broadcasting (CPB) and National Public Radio (NPR). This act is said to have been a major obstacle to the continuing existence of low-power radio because it established new rules for stations to qualify for public funding (Soley, 1999). Prior to the 1967 act, noncommercial radio stations were eligible to apply for federal grants that supported community media. Under the new rules, stations had to have at least five full-time staff members and broadcast at a minimum of 3,000 watts, thus eliminating low power stations from eligibility for federal aid; 80% of the noncommercial stations in 1970 did not qualify for federal assistance (Fornatale & Mills, 1980, pp. 175–176).

In 1978, the FCC adopted a series of new rules (FCC, 1978) governing low-power noncommercial licenses in response to a CPB request to make room for larger noncommercial stations. These rules ended the acceptance of Class D, 10-watt license applications and gave Class D stations a secondary status that subjected them to displacement by larger stations (Stavitsky, 2000). Thus the majority of small, community-accessible radio stations were eventually turned into professional entities, produced and programmed by nonlocal groups. This has resulted in the situation we have in 2004, where public radio stations are increasingly dominated by nonlocal, nationally distributed productions such as "All Things Considered," "A Prairie Home Companion," and "Car Talk."

RESPONSES TO THE FALL OF LOW-POWER RADIO

It was not long after the 1978 FCC ruling that ended the licensing of low-power stations, that activists began to challenge this broadcast policy. In a long tradition of illegal broadcasting (Henry & von Joel, 1984) low-power radio activists began using small transmitters to broadcast signals on unused parts of the spectrum. Mbanna Kantako, a blind African American living in Springfield, Illinois, was credited with "starting" the micro radio movement when he went on the air with a one-watt transmitter November 27,1986, from the living room of his apartment in the John Jay Holmes public housing project (Coopman, 1997; Soley, 1999). WTRA, named after the Tenants Rights Association (TRA) he helped organize, started broadcasting two nights a week, and by 1988 changed its name to "Zoom Black Magic Liberation Radio" to reflect Kantako's vision of raising "the consciousness of the people" (Soley, 1999).

Kantako's micro station, later shortened to "Black Liberation Radio" was significant to this study and the micro radio movement in general because of its role in establishing a coherent, aggressive legal defense of low-power radio. Kantako incurred regular confrontations with local authorities and in 1990 a federal court ordered him to shut down his transmitter. Kantako turned to the National Lawyers Guild Committee on Democratic Communication (NLGCDC) for help. The NLGCDC was "formed in 1987 to explore the applicability of traditional First Amendment concepts in the face of the world wide monopolization of communication resources by commercial interests" (Soley, 1999, p. 75).

Peter Franck, an attorney and co-chair of the NLGCDC, took the case and the defense of micro broadcasters became a ten-year project for the CDC. According to Franck, "this started the ball rolling on legal research on free radio broadcasting" (Soley, 1999, p. 75). The NLGCDC drafted a legal brief to defend Kantako when the FCC decided to shut him down. The FCC delayed enforcement of the court order because no commercial broadcaster had filed an interference complaint against Kantako (Soley, 1999). It was not until 1993 that the NLGCDC put its legal leg work before a judge in a case that established the legal defense of many micro broadcasters to follow.

U.S. V. DUNIFER: A LANDMARK IN LEGAL DISCOURSE FOR MICRO RADIO

The legal decision that set the precedent for the micro radio community was *U.S. v. Dunifer*. Free Radio Berkeley, an illegal micro radio station run by Stephen Dunifer, had received attention in the San Francisco Bay area press in 1993 and 1994. The FCC responded by requesting the forfeiture of Dunifer's broadcast equipment and fining him $20,000. Dunifer filed an administrative appeal arguing in defense of his First Amendment rights, among other things. The FCC failed to respond to the appeal for more than one year. Dunifer continued to broadcast, and the FCC eventually asked the U.S. district court in northern California to issue an emergency injunction to stop his broadcasting. Judge Claudia Wilken denied the injunction and suspended judgment while the government provided more information. Judge Wilken's decision to suspend judgment and delay enforcement of FCC law marked the first time any court had rejected FCC efforts to stop an unlicensed broadcaster from accessing the public airwaves (Korn, 1996). This case drew significant attention to the issues raised by micro broadcasters.

Dunifer made a number of arguments in defending himself against the FCC. There was no dispute about the act of illegal broadcasting. Dunifer, with the help of attorney Louis Hiken of the NLGCDC, acknowledged his actions and made the following arguments in his motion in opposition to the FCC's motion for preliminary injunction (*U.S. v. Dunifer*, 1994):

1. The FCC failed to respond to Dunifer's request for permission to broadcast and should have done so before approaching the courts. Dunifer did not question the Constitutionality of licensing; rather he argued that the failure to issue Class D licenses is not the least restrictive way to regulate the airwaves and is unconstitutional under the overbreadth doctrine of the First Amendment. What Dunifer argued here was that the Communications Act of 1934 mandated the FCC to regulate the airwaves in the "least restrictive

way." Dunifer felt that his broadcasting demonstrated the potential of low-power radio and by outlawing micro radio, the FCC regulation of the broadcast spectrum was overly broad.

2. Dunifer argued the lack of explicit criteria for the acceptance or denial of petitions for waivers to regulations allows random enforcement of the law and does not ensure the equal protection principles of the Fifth Amendment.

3. Dunifer argued that he had not interfered with other broadcasts as evidenced by the delayed enforcement of FCC laws.

4. Shutting down Free Radio Berkeley violated Section 2324 of the Communications Act of 1934, which requires broadcasters to use the "minimum amount of power necessary to carry out the communication desired."

5. The government has the burden of proof to show the defendant is causing "irreparable injury" and failed to do so given that the broadcasts occurred for two years prior to enforcement of the regulations.

These arguments prompted Judge Wilken to respond with a denial of the preliminary injunction and a stay to allow the FCC to address the constitutional issues. She said,

The government has failed to address the Constitutional issues in the FCC forfeiture action and has inadequately addressed them in arguments before this Court . . . in light of current technology, is a total ban on new licensing of micro radio broadcasting the least restrictive means available to protect against chaos in the airwaves? (*U.S. v. Dunifer*, 1995, p. 5)

The FCC responded by arguing that Wilken's court, a District Court in California, does not have jurisdiction to hear arguments about the constitutionality of FCC regulations. All appeals of FCC regulations are supposed to be heard in the U.S. court of appeals in the District of Columbia. In denying a motion for summary judgment and establishing her jurisdiction for this case, Wilken based her ruling on the forfeiture component of the government's case. Wilken ruled that circuit courts *do* have jurisdiction over forfeiture cases (*U.S. v. Dunifer*, 1995). Having established the authority to hear the case, the judge requested further briefing from both parties as to whether "the unconstitutionality of the FCC regulatory scheme would be a valid defense in an action brought by the FCC to enjoin broadcasting without a license" (*U.S. v. Dunifer*, 1997).

In the final opinion in *U.S. v. Dunifer*, the judge acknowledged the merit of Dunifer's case but denied him standing because he had not applied for a broadcast license and been rejected. Usually the plaintiff is required to demonstrate standing, but in the ninth circuit, there was precedent requiring this of defendants who make affirmative defenses that challenge the constitutionality of a government regulation. By failing to go through the application process Dunifer had not exhausted his administrative options prior to the case. Although the FCC does not grant Class D licenses, all of its rules and regulations are subject to appeal and application of a request for waiver. This was a formal process, and the judge found, "Mr. Dunifer's presentation of the constitutional issues in his forfeiture proceeding is not the equivalent of applying for a license and requesting a waiver" (*U.S. v. Dunifer*, 1998a, p. 1240). Because he never applied for the license and waiver, the court said he did not have standing to challenge those regulations.

Although the case ended with Dunifer enjoined from broadcasting, Judge Wilken wrote, "The United States had failed to show a probability of success on the constitutional issues raised by Mr. Dunifer" (*U.S. v. Dunifer*, 1998a), sending a strong signal to both the FCC and the micro broadcasters. This decision revealed a hole in the FCC regulatory scheme; Judge Wilken provided a map on how to get there. The micro broadcast community must first apply for licenses and waivers, and if denied, then make the arguments Dunifer made. Dunifer has since filed an appeal of the 1998 decision.The arguments made in this case have reappeared in the defense of many subsequent micro broadcasters. The summary of this legal case provides a picture of the intricate legal maneuvering by the activists and by the FCC in attempting to enforce broadcast policy and keep low-power broadcasters off the air. The Dunifer case revealed the FCC's position prior to the decision to license LPFM and is a significant piece of the history leading up to the policy change by the FCC.

MICRO RADIO IN THE POPULAR AND ACADEMIC PRESS

Micro radio received increasing attention from writers and researchers in the late 1990s as the FCC moved to license low-power radio. The popular newspaper press featured stories about the FCC closing micro stations and then as the issue progressed, the news media focused more on the intragovernmental struggle that developed between the FCC and the U.S. Congress. This press coverage is examined in detail in Chapter 7. The following summary focuses on the scholarly research on micro radio and a couple of books written by activists. One interesting feature to note among many of these sources is the connection between the academic and the activist communities. The interconnections between these two groups demonstrate the discursive link between these two groups of people. As we will see, the connections between the academic and the activist community were an integral piece that contributed to the emergence of micro radio.

An example of a scholar who is active in the micro radio community is Ted Coopman. He has presented work at conferences and as well as published journal articles on micro radio. Beginning with his master's thesis, "Sailing the Spectrum form Pirates to Micro Broadcasters: A Case Study of Micro Broadcasting in the San Francisco Bay Area" (Coopman, 1995), Coopman explored the evolution of micro radio activism from the hills of Berkeley to the halls of Congress. His initial work detailed the theory and practice of Stephen Dunifer's Free Radio Berkeley and pointed to democratic communication as a larger struggle embodied within the micro radio debate. Coopman (1995) also noted a trend of extreme animosity among micro radio activists toward their opponents. This communication breakdown embodied the contradiction of fighting for free speech as some activists tried to silence their critics. This theme reappears in this study as well, marking a persistent characteristic of a movement and revealing the difficulty of uniting people around an issue as broad as media and democracy.

At the time of his analysis of the struggle between Dunifer and the FCC, Coopman (1998) noted the difference between the micro radio movement and previous pirate radio rebels. Coopman found a gap in understanding between the FCC and the activists and described the FCC as reacting as if micro radio was just another form of illegal broadcasting despite the activist's arguments about the importance of democratic access to communication technology.

The primary proponents of this movement have already committed their lives to pursuing their definition of social justice, and they view micro radio as an important tool in attaining their goals. Thus, the use of radio is not an end to itself, nor is the right of a particular person, Stephen Dunifer, or Richard Edmonson to broadcast. Rather, micro radio is a means to achieving the principle of democratic communication. . . . It is this view of micro radio as a tool of social change that the FCC fails to publicly acknowledge. (Coopman, 1998)

Coopman's early identification of the larger social struggle around micro radio provided a historical reference point by which to judge the findings of this study. As we will see, the FCC in general and FCC Chairman William Kennard in particular eventually came to understand the position of the activists to the point of usurping the role of spokesperson for the movement.

The Internet proved to be a powerful organizing tool for micro radio activists and their on-line communications form a significant piece of this study. Initially, Coopman (2000a) identified dominant web sites (www.radio4all.org) and e-mail tools (MRN Listserv) used by the micro radio activists. Coopman noted:

Without the Internet, and the access and instantaneous communication it affords, this movement likely could not have consolidated and maximized its resources enough to form the significant challenge to the status quo that it is today. Micro radio has gone from being a non-issue in 1995 to both the FCC and NAB having "pirate" information on their websites. (Coopman, 2000a)

Coopman traced the history of these Internet communication tools and argued that the Internet was reconfiguring the way this "free communications movement" was able to act and react. Coopman (2000b) updated this work by examining the coordinating activity that went on among the activists as they worked to come up with statements to submit to the FCC during the FCC's public comment period. Coopman (2000b) noted the record number of public comments submitted to the FCC in response to their initial "Notice of Proposed Rulemaking" (FCC, 1999). Coopman also noted the divisions within the movement and the difficulties faced in trying to reach agreement on the goals to be achiveved. Nevertheless, Coopman attributed the relative success of the micro radio activists to the coordinating possibilities presented by the Internet.

The Micro Radio Movement, largely enabled by the communication abilities of the internet, is transforming into an independent media reform movement and a source of support for activist organizing, and resistance to the dominating forces in American society. (Coopman, 2000b)

Coopman based much of his research on documents and email archives he acquired through his personal involvement in the movement. His enthusiasm for the movement's ability to mobilize people across the country and across the ideological spectrum can be seen in his conclusions about the possibilities for social changes presented by the Internet.

Howley (2000) was another researcher who placed micro radio in the context of social movement activism. He was also another example of an academic scholar who was actively involved with a micro radio station. (Howley taught at Northeastern University and worked with Free Radio Allston, a micro radio station outside of Boston.) Howley found the micro radio struggle to embody larger issues about the nature of democracy, technology and society.

In its efforts to reinvent radio as a vehicle of participatory democracy and a resource for community development, the micro radio community not only demonstrates the medium's significance to our understanding of community, democracy, and citizenship, but underscores the role media activism plays as an agent of progressive social change. (Howley, 2000, p. 257)

Thus Howley connected micro radio to a larger movement of "media activism." This idea is central to this research project. Many of the scholars who have researched micro radio use the word "movement" to describe the work of the activists. The "movement" aspects of micro radio are often assumed or attributed in a loose fashion. This research examines the social movement concept found in much of this literature on micro radio.

Equally persuasive though lacking the scholarly tone, Ruggiero (1999) argued the connections between micro radio and a functioning democracy. Ruggiero was affiliated with "Steal This Radio," a micro station in New York City and was a plaintiff in a lawsuit, *Free Speech v. FCC*, that sough to establish "the airwaves as a public forum and as such a venue where free speech should be protected by the Constitution" (Ruggiero, 1999, pp. 28–29). Ruggiero provided an overview of the issues involved in the micro radio struggle along with some practical information about how to support micro radio. He also placed micro radio in the context of a larger social struggle, invoking a civil rights discourse that we will see reappear among the activists as they represent their story to the press (see Chapter 7).

Like Rosa Parks, we are not willing to wait for court cases or petition results to sit in the front of the airwaves. As enormous corporations merge and rival nation states for real global power, regaining control of communications at the local level represents a genuine revolution, a grassroots insurgency to advance our basic human freedoms and to place public access to communications at the heart of our everyday lives. (Ruggiero, 1999, p. 42)

Thus media access was likened to a basic human right, the right to be able to represent ones own community *to* ones community. This articulation of the larger issues embedded within micro radio is another indication of the cognitive terrain that was developed by the media activists as they worked to advance this specific cause. With a forward by McChesney and quotes from Noam Chomsky and others, Ruggiero's work draws on a history of scholarship and ideas that about the relationship between media and society. Micro radio became an opportunity for those ideas to gain renewed public exposure.

Not all scholars who have researched micro radio have been so optimistic about the future of the media and democracy movement. Jassem (2000) examined the concept of localism in broadcast history and questioned whether pirate radio would eventually add any real local content. Like Stavisky's (1994) work on localism, Jassem found changing conceptions of localism. The local was said to include the geographically proximate as well as communities of interest groups. These changing notions of community, coupled with the emergence of Internet radio, digital radio and cable and direct satellite radio, created barriers to the significant contribution purported by micro radio advocates.

For the future, if localism matters, it isn't at all clear that pirate radio will be a necessary or significant part of it on radio . . . though it is clear that content and structure are related, one does not guarantee the other. In other words, "more" radio outlets, even low powered ones, may or may not yield programming that would be considered "local." (Jassem, 2000, p. 24)

Jassem did not assume the pirates would remain committed to local issues and culture. He then offered a qualified assessment of their potential contribution to the "local" content of broadcast media. With similarly unenthusiastic findings, Dick and McDowell (2000, 2001) found the micro radio community to have evolved from rabid antigovernment fanatics into more "professional" broadcasters. This evolution is said to be a response to the FCC initiative to license LPFM. Dick and McDowell (2001) assign the changes among the activists community to a belief that the FCC will eventually license LPFM despite current congressional opposition. The changes notwithstanding, Dick and McDowell (2001) reached tentative conclusions about the future contribution of micro radio and its possibilities for contributing to democratic media reform.

Legal scholars have taken up the micro broadcasting issue as a number of court cases have gained national attention. Alan Korn of the National Lawyers Guild argued that the U.S. Congress's failure to respond to calls for expanding access to public airwaves has moved the battle into the courtroom. "If micro radio receives legitimacy in the future, it will be because hundreds of broadcasters engaged in principled acts of civil disobedience, despite threats of substantial fines and criminal penalties" (Korn, 1996, p. 53). Supporting this view were a number of recent position papers on the topic. A 1998 paper presented to the National Association of Broadcasters (NAB) called on the NAB to support the licensing of small, low power radio stations, declaring "The NAB has a historic opportunity to show the world that it too is committed to the Constitution and democracy, and to the sharing of the electronic spectrum between the commercial broadcast industry and democracy at the grassroots" (Franck, 1998, p. 4). Similarly, work by Jesse Walker, an independent researcher on this topic, has advocated easing FCC regulation as a way to promote public access to the airwaves. Walker wrote,

As Congress considers its options with regard to public broadcasting, it ought to think about starting by making micro radio legal. And not just legal: the long delays, the heavy paperwork, the expensive legal labor involved in starting a new station should be slashed. The best way to do that would be for the FCC to simply allow stations that broadcast over unused frequencies to continue as those frequencies' common-law owners, stepping in only when they interfere with another operator's signal. (Walker, 1997, p. 23)

This analysis confronts the current FCC policy that has set a high financial entry fee for use of the broadcast spectrum. Class C license applications require engineering studies, legal services and equipment estimated to cost over $250,000. Also, the "system of competitive bidding" used to award licenses raises the costs considerably. Walker argued these policies limit access to the public airwaves to those with enough money to buy and run a powerful radio station. Walker also advocated the licensing of small, 10-watt stations and the setting space aside on the broadcast spectrum for these stations as a way of democratizing the airwaves. Also, a 1998 three-part series of position papers from the Freedom Forum documented the recent debate over micro radio and made recommendations similar to Walker's (Taylor, 1998).

   Two books on micro radio come straight out of the movement and provide first-hand accounts of the strategies and tactics employed by people engaged in the practice of illegal micro broadcasting. First, a collection of essays, *Seizing the Airwaves: A Free Radio Handbook*, was published in 1998 by a small California press. The essays range from philosophical pieces about broadcasting and democracy to personal accounts of activists within the movement. This book included an essay by Robert McChesney that led off the collection and outlined the political and economic history of the allocation of broadcast licenses. McChesney wrote,

Both Democratic and Republican parties have strong ties to large communication firms and industries, and the communication lobbies are among the most feared, respected and well endowed of all that seek favors on Capitol Hill. . . . The debate over communications policy is restricted to the elites and those with serious financial stakes in the outcome. It does not reflect well on the caliber of U.S. participatory democracy, but it is capitalist democracy at its best. (Sakolsky & Dunifer, 1998, p. 24)

McChesney's essay and his previous scholarship (McChesney, 1993, 1997, 1999, 2002b) combined with the first-person perspectives of many of the leading proponents of micro radio, provided a detailed description of the political and legal position of these "pirates" and the issues they were addressing. The presence of McChesney coupled with the background of the editors (Stephen Dunifer was a leading micro radio advocate and distributor of the tools and knowledge to go on the air and Ron Sakolsky was a researcher and professor) marks another case where the academy and movement activists linked up to create a complex set of concepts and skills to advance micro radio in particular and media activism in general.

Another in-depth case study of the people and practices involved with micro radio came from Richard Edmondson, the founder of San Francisco Liberation Radio and an active member of the micro radio activist community. Edmondson's book, *Rising Up: Class Warfare in America from the Streets to the Airwaves*, chronicled the history of San Francisco Liberation Radio, the connections to the local nonprofit human rights groups, "Food Not Bombs" and the FCC enforcement that shut down the station. Edmondson saw the micro radio struggle as a class war with the poor fighting for a piece of the broadcast spectrum.

Consider the irony: here we were at the end of the 20th century. Suddenly the FCC, which has been licensing stations in this country since 1934, considers a rule change which would allow poor people to operate their own inexpensive, low power radio stations . . . the rich broadcasters are not going to willingly give up their vast holdings. Presumably neither will the poor be satisfied with the proverbial crumbs for which they have always settled. The stage would thus be set for a class war—fought over the airwaves, with freedom of speech as the prize. (Edmondson, 2000, p. xvi)

Edmondson applied a strict class based model of broadcast regulation and described first hand accounts of the effort to give the homeless a media voice. This case study of local community media was an in-depth study of the issues media activists faced on the ground as they worked to serve a marginalized population.

One interesting note about the books by Edmondson and Dunifer was their geographic origin. Although the press, the FCC, and activists themselves noted micro stations all across the station, the two most recent books on the subject originated from the San Francisco Bay area of California. The public-ation of micro radio issues by Dunifer and Edmondson is one measure of their role as de-facto leaders in a somewhat leaderless movement. These books, in combination with web sites and e-mail lists, served as sites were the knowledge generated by the activists was codified and distributed to a larger audience.

Finally, the wider connections between alternative media and social movements have received increased scholarly attention in the late 1990s. A number of scholars have demonstrated renewed interest in alternative, independent media and have further theorized the connections between participatory communication and democracy (Atton, 2001; Couldry, 2000; Downing, 2001; Fairchild, 2001; Halleck, 2001; Hamilton, 2000; Dagron, 2001). In particular, *Making Waves: Stories of Participatory Communication for Social Change* is a collection of essays about community media from around the world. Written as a report to the Rockefeller Foundation by Alfonso Dagron (2001), it examines the impact of community media on international development and drew attention to two pieces important aspects of participatory communication: power and identity. "The democratization of communication cuts through the issue of power. Participatory approaches contribute to put decision-making in the hands of the people" (Dagron, 2001, p. 34). The second component of this conceptualization of participatory communication was the role in Identity. Identity had a long history of research from Cultural Studies to Anthropology and in this case was connected to community media.

Especially in communities that have been marginalized, repressed or simply neglected over decades, participatory communication contributes to instilling cultural pride and self-esteem. It reinforces the social tissue through the strengthening of local and indigenous forms of organization. (Dagron, 2001, p. 34)

Local media was then argued to be a force for social cohesion among groups that were not represented by the dominant media. This issue of exclusion from media, what has been call symbolic annihilation, emerged as the theme of diversity among the activists as they developed a discourse about micro radio.

In *Radical Media: Rebellious Communication and Social Movements*, Downing (2001) made the case for the importance of alternative communication to a variety of social movements. Downing drew attention to the connections between "radical media" and a host of social movements, though he did not make the case for alternative media *as* a social movement. Downing attributed a central role in the process of social change to social movements.

Parties legislate, but they do not generally initiate or lead major movements of social opinion. This means that the political life energy and the burning issues of a nation are more often to be found in and around social movements than in the official institutions of democracy. (Downing, 2001, p. 26)

Downing summarized a number of cases of "radical media," including micro radio, noting the persistence of these media regardless of the rise of fall of a social movement. Downing also pointed out the use of alternative media by repressive organizations as well as progressive groups. Thus radical media, from graffiti to micro radio embody a wide set of communication tools that have been employed by social movements. One area Downing did not address was the question of media activism as a social movement.

The idea of media activism and reform as a stand alone social movement has gained increasing acceptance. McChesney and Nichols wrote the lead article in a January 2002 issue of the *Nation* titled, "The Making of a Movement: Getting Serious about Media Reform" and these arguments and ideas grew into the book, *Our Media Not Theirs: The Democratic Struggle against Corporate Media* (McChesney & Nichols, 2002b). In their book, McChesney and Nichols speak directly about the possibilities of organizing popular opinion to raise awareness about the need for democratic access to media technologies. *Our Media Not Theirs* is the clearest articulation to date of a media activism and reform movement and marks a growing acceptance of the idea of an emerging social movement around media reform and democracy.

Given this overview of the history and scholarship of the development of the micro radio movement, let us now turn to the larger cultural, political and economic context in which this movement was operating, including changing broadcast policy and the trends associated with neo-liberalism/late capitalism/post-fordist economy.

NEW SOCIAL MOVEMENT THEORY

The micro radio movement is one piece of a larger field of media activism. From First Amendment lawyers to conservative Christians, the micro radio community united diverse constituents behind a specific goal of broadcast policy reform. This ideologically diverse movement embodied many of the characteristics associated with new social movements (NSM). New social movement theory can help us understand the micro radio movement and allow us to place the tactics and strategies into the larger context of social movements in general.

Alberto Melucci is one of the primary theorists behind new social movement theory. He is less concerned with the distinction of "new" as opposed to "old" and more interested in asking questions that are appropriate to our changing complex society. Melucci noted three significant changes in society that warrant a reconception of how social movements are viewed. First, the United States and the Western world at large have moved from a resource-based economy to an information-based economy. The transformation of nature into commodities requires the creation, distribution and maintenance of cultural codes that reinforce that transformation. Melucci writes,

Our access to reality is facilitated and shaped by the conscious production and control of information. "Forms" or images produced through perception and cognition increasingly organize our relationship to the material and communicative environment in which we live. The transformation of natural resources into commodities has come to depend on the production and control of the cognitive and communicative forms. (Melucci, 1989, p. 185)

Thus, communication media has become a central component of our current economic and social system.

Second, we have reached a stage where we are operating at a planetary level. Nothing is outside the system. There is no place to hide. More and more of the natural environment and diverse cultures of the world are being opened up to the influences of global market forces. Third, the primary actors in this system are individuals, unattached to political parties, religions, or civic groups. "The main actors within the system are no longer groups defined by class consciousness, religious affiliation, or ethnicity" (Melucci, 1989, p. 185). Melucci argues that these changes necessitate new questions about our society and new ways of thinking about how people organize themselves to address issues of social change.

Melucci hypothesized four characteristics of NSMs. First, they are information based. These new movements are more about confronting the creation of cultural codes than they are about struggles over access to resources. Second, these movements take a planetary perspective, creating unforeseen alliances. He cites the work of middle class college kids in the 1980s to end Apartheid in South Africa, half a world away. A more recent example would be the anti-sweatshop movement currently active on college campuses. These middle-class students are not fighting for the protection of their parents' manufacturing jobs but rather for the protection of workers they have never met and probably never will. Third, Melucci believes NSMs spend a significant amount of time building community as opposed to protesting. This community becomes a model of the changes sought: organized around equity with shared power and consensus decision making. "Living differently and changing society are seen as complementary" (Melucci, 1989, p. 206). NSMs are said to encourage a merging of the public and private in such a way that new lifestyles becomes integrated into the cause. It is as much a goal to live differently as it is to participate in any militant protest. The NSM idea is to live the cause, embody the change as much as you advocate it. Finally, Melucci argued that NSMs "display the seeds of a new awareness of the global dimensions of complex societies" (Melucci, 1989, p. 206). This awareness is said to include cultural diversity as well as biological diversity, acknowledging that the "human species is a fully interdependent human and natural world system" (Melucci, 1989, p. 206).

In addition to these features, NSMs are said to cut across ideological lines, no longer restricted to the boundaries of class. Also, they often have specific, particular, short-term goals as opposed to the older model of large-scale "revolution." NSMs rely on identity for participation and often help to create or advance identities through participation, such as becoming more of a self-identified environmentalist after blocking the road to a timber sale. The wide range of issues addressed by NSMs is said to be a reaction to globalization, where "post-Fordism inevitably introduces a new series of antagonisms that motivate collective action" (Escobar, 1992, p. 78).

This study is based on a model of social movements proposed by Eyerman and Jamison (1991). Eyerman and Jamison propose a cognitive approach that draws on the work of Melucci and Escobar, as well as work from the sociological school of resource mobilization theory (Zald & McCarthy, 1987; Touraine, 1981). Attempting to integrate the contributions of the various strains of social movement research, Eyerman and Jamison argue that social movements are sites of knowledge production. That knowledge is described as a "cognitive terrain," explored by activists and distributed to the larger society through the course of movement activity. Successful movements fade into the background as their knowledge becomes integrated into the dominant institutions and conceptions of society. Citing Touraine in their conception of social movements, Eyerman and Jamison write, "For Touraine a social movement, as distinct from a protest organization or mobilization campaign, is characterized by the realization of historicity, by the self-conscious awareness that the very foundations of society are at stake in the contest" (Eyerman & Jamison, 1991, p. 27). Thus, Eyerman and Jamison found the environmental movement to have made major contributions to the way people thought about life on earth, having essentially "re-cognized" awareness about humans relationship to nature. Social movements are said to produce both knowledge and practice, what Eyerman and Jamison call "cognitive praxis."

Throughout this study the terms "cognitive terrain" and "cognitive praxis" are used to describe the work of the media activists. These terms are borrowed from Eyerman and Jamison (1991) and refer to the process of individual knowledge that is then shaped by social interaction. The word cognitive is used to draw attention to the role of the individual's own thoughts and feelings. The term praxis is meant to imply agency and a social process that includes interaction with other actors. This social interaction is said to help shape the outward expression of individuals' thoughts, feelings and actions. Thus, activists may rely on his or her personal knowledge of a subject as the basis for their opinions (cognitive information) yet the action they take to address that subject (praxis) is the product of a social context that is "neither predetermined nor completely self-willed; its meaning is derived form the context in which it is carried out" (p. 3). Thus "cognitive praxis" will be used to describe the work of the activist community and cognitive terrain will be used to describe the range of ideas that the activists explored in pursuit of micro radio. Chapter 1 expands on this cognitive model of new social movements and applies this model to the emerging movement of media activism.

Finally, this study is grounded in a poststructural paradigm where significant social struggle is said to manifest around issues of language, representation and communication. Discourse is a term used throughout this research as a concept that invokes this poststructural paradigm. Use of the term discourse in this study has roots back to a tradition established by Michel Foucault (1977). Foucault used discourse to mean the "collective habits of talk, action, and interpretation embedded in historical contexts that establish and enact relations of power and resistance" (Streeter, 1996, p. xiii). Thus the discourse picked up and deployed by the activist community in their pursuit of micro radio embodied "relations of power and resistance." Discourse is a system of linguistic and symbolic tools embedded with possibility and constraints that provide resources for action but also impose limits on that action. Discourses often rely on language and signs that carry with them a previous history that can both enable and inhibit the possibility for new meanings. Because of the theoretical connections between NSMs and information, analysis of communication is central to the study of a new social movement such as the media activism and reform movement. Discourse analysis offers a set of theoretical and methodological tools for researching the communication process.

This research is grounded in the work of Norman Fairclough. Fairclough has published a number of books about critical discourse analysis (CDA) and has articulated specific theoretical and methodological ideas for research using this technique. Fairclough (1992, 1995) begins with the assumption that discourse is a social practice. He argues that language always plays a role in shaping three things: (1) our social identity, (2) our social relations, and (3) our systems of knowledge and beliefs. As a practice, discourse is constitutive of the social, that is, shaped by social relations while at the same time shaping those relations.

NEW SOCIAL MOVEMENTS AND MICRO RADIO

Given this definition of NSMs, this theoretical lens is especially useful for understanding media activism in general and micro radio in particular. Media activism is first and foremost about information and communication. It is about the active struggle over cultural codes and the democratizing of the process whereby we come to understand our world. Micro radio activists emphasize the importance of access to communication technology. It is through the media that society communicates across great distances, geographically and ideologically. When participation in that conversation is limited to the few and the professionals willing to work for media conglomerates, the engine of cultural production is left to those with profit in mind. Micro radio activism is also responding to the globalization of the media networks, where eight corporations now dominate the cultural and political fare of the planet. Following the NSM model, micro radio activism draws on the work on thousands of loosely knit individuals. When these individuals act in concert, they appear to be able to move a force the size of the FCC.

Chapter 1 presents a typology for the media activism and reform movement in the United States at the turn of the millennium. The typology begins the process of identifying the pieces and players that make up the growing social response to media technology and ownership in the twenty-first century. Other scholars have discussed alternative media and have made some connections with social movements, but as of yet there have been no significant attempts to map the growing interest in issues of media and democracy, media access, and free communications. This typology attempts to map out some preliminary parameters to the media activism and reform movement and then looks closely at how this movement took part in the struggle over micro radio.

Chapters 2 and 3 are detailed examinations of the messy process inside a social movement as participants attempt to explore the cognitive terrain of media activism. Using three years (1998–2000) of historical archive of the micro radio network (MRN) listserv, these chapters examine the process of establishing effective discursive formations with which to promote micro radio and the process of identifying the opponents (the Other) and deciding on strategies for responding to those opponents. The listserv archive is a unique historical archive that reads much like a conversation. In previous eras, discussions such as these would have been lost to the ethers or recorded as meeting minutes as best. This Internet technology allowed activists nationwide to share information instantly and respond to issues and ideas as they emerged.

Chapter 4 examines the dominant newspaper coverage of micro radio for three years, 1998–2000. It documents one of the ways that movement knowledge was moved from the periphery of the movement and onto the kitchen table of middle American. This news coverage demonstrated a consistency with the MRN listserv, with many of the same people and organizations represented in both media. The news coverage also demonstrated the unique types of information contributed by representatives of the three categories within the typology proposed in Chapter 1.

Chapters 5 and 6 examine the governmental documents in which the micro radio discourse was codified. The FCC "Report and Order" establishing the micro radio licensing scheme consistently recognized the arguments made by the activists and used those arguments in part to establish new broadcast regulations. In contrast, the debate in Congress became an intragovernmental struggle over who had the authority to propose new broadcast regulations, the FCC or Congress?

This study traces the discourse of the media activism and reform movement as it coalesced around the issue of micro radio. The story of micro radio is not over and the influence of media activism is just beginning. As we move into the heart of the information age, social struggle over media technology will continue to be at the forefront of efforts to address social justice issues. Media and social change are intimately connected and media activists are just beginning to learn to speak truth to the power of broadcasting.

1

A Typology for Media Activism: A Social Movement about Media and Democracy

This chapter presents a typology for a significant social movement that has emerged at the close of the twentieth century: media activism. Similar to any social movement, media activism is a heterogeneous movement drawing on a range of skills and agendas, uniting people across the social and political spectrum. In thinking about the environmental movement for a moment, it is apparent that there is a wide range of groups taking on a host of issues with a variety of tactics. From the grassroots environmentalists of Earth First! who use direct action in an attempt to stop individual acts of logging or mining to the more institutional Sierra Club that prefers congressional lobbying for policy change, the environmental movement relies on a host of strategies and tactics to achieve its goals. From lawyers to lobbyists, radical tree sitters to public interest scientists, the environmental movement encompasses a wide diversity of skill sets and agendas. The environmental movement as a whole can be subdivided into smaller categories, from deep ecology to environmental justice. Although these smaller, more focused areas of the environmental movement are narrowly tailored to their specific issue, they still fall under the large umbrella of the environmental movement.

In many ways parallel to the environmental movement, media activism embodies a diverse mix of people and approaches focused around confronting and critiquing the consolidated media conglomerates that dominate the global landscape at the turn of the millennium.

A social movement is not one organization or one particular interest group. It is more like a cognitive territory, a conceptual space that is filled by dynamic interactions between different groups and organizations. (Eyerman & Jamison, 1991, p. 55)

From independent media production and distribution to nonprofit media policy think tanks, activists, lawyers, citizens, and scholars are confronting the current media establishment in increasingly visible ways. The diversity of this movement, as with any social movement, makes the process of mapping the entire movement difficult if not impossible. Although every aspect of the movement is not easily catalogued, significant areas of movement activity can be identified. By establishing a typology of media activism, general categories of activity can be identified that reveal the types of strategies and tactics being used as well as the interactions among the various categories of participants. (See Figure 1.1.)

Media activism is a growth industry. From media literacy to independent media production, individuals and groups are using new technology to create, critique, and communicate about media. A typical Internet search for "media activism" yields hundreds of viable web sites for groups and individuals interested in the broad topic. Seventy-five or more links to media activist organizations can be found on the more prominent web sites such as Fairness and Accuracy in the Media (FAIR) or Project Censored. In addition, the fall of 2002 saw a number of information campaigns and conferences focused on issues of media democracy and reform, including the International Media Democracy Day (www.mediademocracyday.org) and the newly formed Action Coalition for Media Education (www.acmecoalition.org). Similarly, there has been a global proliferation of IndyMedia (www.indymedia.org) web sites that have attempted to circumvent the gatekeeper function of corporate media (Downing, 2003; Kidd, 2003). Since its inception in 1990 during the World Trade Organization protests in Seattle, close to 100 IndyMedia sites have sprung up in over forty countries worldwide. These organizations are often interactive with one another, and highly interactive with their members through the use of e-mail listservs. Their increasing visibility over the past few years is yet another sign of this emerging social movement.

Although there has been a dramatic proliferation of media watchdog groups, independent media production, and commentary about the media in the last decade, the scholarly community is just beginning to define the proliferation of media activism. Most recently, McChesney and Nichols (2002b) have described the nascent media movement. "We want to fan the flames of the movement for media reform that we believe is taking shape in the United States. . . . In some respects, the United States is a laggard in the global media reform movement and we have much to learn from studying other nations and working with them" (p. 44). McChesney and Nichols are some of the first (and most visible scholars in the United States) to describe media activism as a movement and they link the activity in this country to a global effort to address public access to communication technology.

Some are calling it the "media and democracy" movement, others the "free communications movement." In *The Progressive Guide to Alternative Media and Activism* Peter Phillips wrote:

In the past several years there have been increased grassroots organizing around issues of media and democracy; from Z magazine's annual Z Media Institute and the formation of groups like the Grassroots News Network, the Direct Action Media Network, and the New

York Free Media Alliance, to two Cultural Environment conventions and two Media and Democracy Congresses.

"Media and Democracy" has become a grassroots movement based on a shared vision of building alternative news and information systems independent from corporate influence. (Phillips, 1999, pp. 10–11)

We the Media: A Citizen's Guide to Fighting for Media and Democracy is another recent text that addresses the ideas of media activism. In the introduction Don Hazen, the Director of the Institute for Alternative Journalism, writes:

We have to resist media which undermines our democracy and our soul and say yes to media that empowers us to participate in civic life and stimulates our active creativity. Some people are calling the growing effort to fight the media powers a "media and democracy" movement. Others are calling it common sense. Whatever it is called, one basic step includes holding our elected officials and the media companies accountable. (Hazen & Winokur, 1997, pp. 1–2)

Regardless of the term, media activism, media and democracy, or free communications, all refer to a large umbrella of issues and organizations addressing the role of the media in the modern world. Although this project is not focused on defining "media activism," it is focused on a specific site of media activism: micro radio. By establishing a broad frame for the terrain of media activism, the specific social actors who are taking part in the micro radio debate can be seen in the context of a larger social movement.

Just as the environmental movement mobilized a wide variety of resources around the issue of preserving the Arctic National Wildlife Refuge, for example, the media activist movement actively engaged in the micro radio debate. Although one might be tempted to identify a "movement " to save the Arctic Refuge, in reality the refuge was a site where the skills, resources, and strategies of the larger, complex, shifting, heterogeneous environmental movement were brought to bear. Thus any discourse that developed around defending the refuge was largely shaped by the interaction of the many pieces of a preexisting environmental movement. Defense of the refuge did not arise out of thin air but rather resulted from the work of grassroots groups, institutional groups and academic discourses already in place and interacting with one another. The same can be said for micro radio and its connections to a larger community of scholars, activists and media makers who are working on issues of media and democracy.

Micro radio and the media issues embodied in this struggle do not constitute a social movement in and of themselves. Instead, micro radio and the discourses that developed to promote the revival of this technology were taking place in the context of a larger social movement of media activism or media and democracy. "No social movement emerges until there is a political context of communication, opening up the potential for problem articulation and knowledge dissemination" (Eyerman & Jamison, 1991, p. 56). In this case, micro radio provided a powerful site where "knowledge dissemination" could take place, and the broader issue of the role of media in a democracy could be brought forward for public discussion. The specific site of micro radio provides a location where many of the issues raised by the media activism movement gained widespread public visibility. The diversity of the groups that participated in the micro radio effort in the United States demonstrates the diversity of the media activism and reform movement at large. Hackett (2000) notes the importance of diversity in his exploration of the emerging media reform movement:

Media democratization is too big a project to be accomplished though any single strategy; and there are potential synergies between different approaches. For example, "those who focus directly on existing power structures and those who work to foster alternatives beyond them expand each others' social wiggle-room." (Hackett, 2000)

Hackett addresses the question of "democracy" in the media movement in his attempt to analyze this emerging social phenomenon.

Given the breadth of issues falling under the rubric of media activism, this book will use the term media activism and reform movement. The more limited term "media reform" used by McChesney and Nichols (2002b) fails to capture the creative, radical participatory nature of activity such as IndyMedia, 'zine production or culture jamming. While policy reform appears to be a central component of this emerging movement, the phrase "be the media" is also a visible slogan and practice that emphasizes agency and direct action that bypasses centralized structures that need reform. Similarly, the term "media and democracy" has a political association that may not apply to the anarchist impulses of radical independent media production. Democracy can imply majority rule and in many cases it is the voices of the minority that are cultivated by alternative media. Clearly no definitive term has solidified and this book adds to the ongoing process of movement formation by attempting to witness the nascent media activism and reform movement as it manifested around the issue of micro radio in the United States.

AN OVERVIEW OF A TYPOLOGY FOR MEDIA ACTIVISM

Figure 1.1 is a proposal for a typology of media activism. The three umbrella categories, individuals and grassroots organizations (GROs), institutional (NGOs), and academic discourses are the general types of groups involved in independent media creation and critique. The boundaries between these categories are fluid, with many organizations combining grassroots elements with academic dialogue or established institutional structure. Although there is significant communication across these categories, there is also communication that often remains confined within the limited realms of the individual categories. Examples of this include academic journals with small audiences that address issues of the political economy of media or media literacy in a technical language such that the knowledge contained in these journals primarily circulates within academic circles. Similarly, public policy think tanks may publish reports on FCC policy that are read by politicians and academics but rarely

Figure 1.1
Typology of Players in the Media Activism Movement

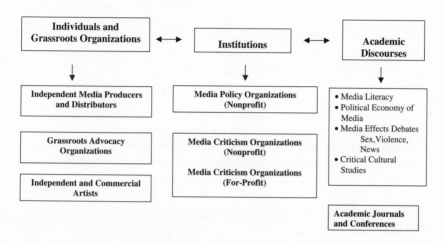

reach a wider grassroots audience. And finally, independent media production, culture jamming, 'zine publishing or even graffiti at the local level may go unseen by the scholars and critics working within more institutional settings. Thus, while many ideas do circulate within and between these categories, there is enough "meme-ic isolation[1] to warrant the identification of specific categories as opposed to a unified homogeneous movement landscape.

The three categories in Figure 1.1 are important because of the distinct work that is accomplished by individuals and groups within each category. Action within each category takes a different form, often has a different audience, and relies upon vastly different skills and knowledge sets. In the first category, individuals and grassroots organizations (GROs), we often find highly committed activists who are willing to attend protests or picket lines, carry signs, chant, cheer, chain themselves to a piece of logging equipment, stay seated on a bus, start an illegal micro radio station, and make puppets. These acts of civil disobedience often elicit media coverage, sometimes positive, sometimes not. Web sites and e-mail lists are increasingly used to unite individuals acting on the grassroots level, allowing them to share knowledge, resources and organize gatherings. Useful knowledge that is exchanged ranges from protest organization, policy updates, conference planning, strategies for dealing with pepper spray and police tactics, and practical skills of media making (e.g., 'zines, web sites, videos, radio).

In the second category, institutions (NGOs), we often find more formal organizations with full time employees who work exclusively on a single issue or cluster of related issues. This policy work is often supported by grants and can include the lobbying of businesses and government bodies in an attempt to effect change. These can be nonprofit as well as commercial organizations that monitor and attempt to influence government legislation and regulations. Useful skills in this category include versatility with the legal system, computer skills and statistical analysis, grant writing, and research. Often these institutions remain out of sight, appearing as sources in newspaper articles or submitting briefs to government bodies. Increasingly these institutions are maintaining regular contact with a support base through e-mail, initiating letter writing campaigns, or "action alerts" about pending decisions or recent atrocities.

The third category in the typology includes institutional as well as public intellectuals. Academic discourse includes the work of scholars and teachers who engage in research across a broad range of subjects using diverse theories and methods. Unlike a policy researcher, academics often address subjects that do not easily translate into immediate policy. From history to philosophy, academic research can yield information that is integral to media activism. The ideas generated by academic discourse circulate through books and journals, at conferences and in the classroom. The structure of disciplinary boundaries within the academy often limits the scope and the audience of academic research. Academics often posses theoretical and methodological research skills, as well as teaching, speaking, and writing skills. Without the direct attachment to policy or a particular government agency, academics are free to pursue subjects that may appear obscure, yet often result in important insights into the human condition or the organization of society. Academic research and theory building often under girds arguments and positions taken up by other activists and public policy institutions.

A TYPOLOGY OF MEDIA ACTIVISM ON MICRO RADIO: INDIVIDUALS AND GRASSROOTS ORGANIZATIONS (GROS)

Specific groups focused on the micro radio issue can be identified in an attempt to flesh out the media activism typology as it pertains to this particular issue (see Figure 1.2). Beginning with individuals and grassroots organizations (GROs), the most basic pieces of the micro radio community are the micro broadcasters themselves. A long list of illegal stations can be found at www.radio4all.org. Many of these stations maintain web sites that provide programming schedules, station news, updates about micro radio issues, technical support and information about recent FCC enforcement actions and direct threats to the stations. The programming formats of these stations range from music to talk, community affairs to government conspiracy. Many of the people who run these stations have been fined and arrested for their civil disobedience and illegal broadcasting. Another example of a grassroots organization involved in the micro radio issue is The Prometheus Radio Project (http://prometheus.tao.ca). According to their web site, The Prometheus Project is designed "to serve as a micro radio resource center offering legal, technical, and organizational support for the non-commercial community broadcasters." Prometheus promotes itself as a defender of the activists who have practiced the civil disobedience that occurred before and during the FCC's move to legalize micro radio. The Prometheus web site states: "Our concern is that those who have fought so hard to make the legalized service possible will be squeezed out by other interests with deeper pockets" (http://prometheus.tao.ca). Another example of an issue-focused grassroots organization is the Mi-

Figure 1.2
Typology for the Media Activism Movement as
Applied to Micro Radio

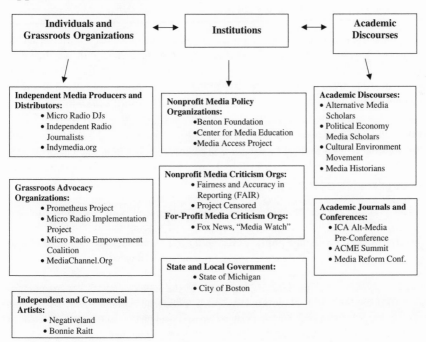

cro Radio Implementation Project (MIP). According to their web site (www.microradio.org/mission.htm), MIP is a "national initiative to assist faith groups, community organizations, multicultural/multiracial populations, linguistic groups, and other nonprofit civil sectors or municipally minded entities in establishing noncommercial low power FM stations." Both the MIP and Prometheus emphasize their commitment to "non-profit" or "non-commercial" broadcasters, pointing to the desire for an alternative to profit-driven media as a central theme of the micro radio activists.

In the same vein, the Microradio Empowerment Coalition (MEC) attempts to unite the many grassroots and more institutional organizations committed to advancing micro radio. In conjunction with the National Lawyers Guild Committee on Democratic Communications, MEC serves as a clearinghouse offering technical assistance to micro broadcasters who want start a station or bureaucratic assistance for those broadcasters applying to the FCC for low-power licenses. The MEC web site states,

We are founded on the principle that democracy depends on community access to information and culture and that access is only genuinely achieved when there exist communications media that are noncommercial, accessible, based in and responsive to the diverse local forces which characterize every community. Building, supporting, and expanding a non-commercial media system is essential to helping to building, supporting and expanding a democratic society. Only with a real democracy will we ever move toward a just and fair society. (http://www.nlgcdc.org/mec/index.html)

Again we see a commitment to noncommercial media, situated within a larger context of "a democratic society." Democracy, commercialism and the public interest are themes that are struggled over by the many stakeholders in this debate. These brief statements from some of the leading grassroots organizations involved in this issue presage the linguistic and ideological struggle fought over micro radio within the broader domain of media activism. These groups are a couple of examples of GROs performing a particular type of work in this portion of the movement typology. Many similar groups exist and this brief summary is intended to be exemplary, not exhaustive.

INSTITUTIONS (NGOs)

The next category in the typology of media activism (Figure 1.2) is institutions (NGOs). The Benton Foundation is an example of a nonprofit media policy organization working to change public policy and raise awareness across a host of media issues. On their web site the Benton Foundation is described as a group that

works to realize the social benefits made possible by the public interest use of communications. Bridging the worlds of philanthropy, public policy, and community action, Benton seeks to shape the emerging communications environment and to demonstrate the value of communications for solving social problems. (http://www.Benton.org)

Started in 1948, the Benton Foundation is dedicated to "exploring the potential of new communications technologies and techniques to help solve social problems" (http://www.Benton.org/About/history.html). With an extensive web site, media news archive and a daily "Communications Headlines" e-mail news service distributed for free, the Benton Foundation combines inside-the-beltway communications policy lobbying and analysis with public outreach in an attempt to increase public awareness and participation in the media policy making process.

Often working in cooperation with the Benton Foundation, the Media Access Project (MAP) is a twenty-seven-year-old nonprofit, public interest telecommunications law firm "which through its programs promotes the public's First Amendment right to hear and be heard on the electronic media of today and tomorrow." (http://www.mediaaccess.org/about). MAP has worked closely with micro radio broadcasters and community groups who attempted to gain broadcast licenses. In addition, they maintain a web site with extensive micro radio resources including original research such as a recent study on the declining presence of local news on television. MAP describes themselves as

the only Washington-based organization devoted to representing listeners' and speakers' interests on electronic media and telecommunications issues before the Federal Communications Commission, other policy-making bodies, and in the courts. (http://www.mediaaccess.org/about)

Again we see an emphasis on nonprofit, public interest work as the focus of the many organizations involved in the micro radio issue.

In the area of nonprofit media criticism organizations, Fairness and Accuracy in Reporting (FAIR) has been particularly supportive of the micro radio initiative. Started in 1986, FAIR works to "invigorate the First Amendment by advocating for greater diversity in the press and by scrutinizing media practices that marginalize public interest, minority and dissenting viewpoints" (www.fair.org). FAIR maintains contact with a network of activists and citizens through a listserv where "action alerts" are posted that call attention to specific stories or reporting practices. It focuses on the news media with the belief that a free and healthy democracy requires the open exchange of information from a variety of sources. "The villain we see is not a person or group, but a historical trend: the increasing concentration of the U.S. media in fewer and fewer corporate hands" (www.fair.org). Thus FAIR embodies a commitment to the public interest in the face of concentrated media, themes repeated throughout the discourse of the media activism movement.

As the information age has come into full bloom, media analysis and critique has moved beyond the classrooms of journalism schools and the pages of obscure academic journals and special interest newsletters. Media criticism has become big business and the economic success of that criticism reflects a broad social interest in meta-commentary, news about news. Examples of this include Fox News Channel's weekly program, "Fox News Watch," where panelists critique and evaluate the media coverage of weekly news stories. One of the weekly panelists is Jeff Cohen, the co-founder of FAIR. Thus media criticism has gained a certain level of entertainment value, occupying space across a range of commercial and noncommercial news outlets.

ACADEMIC DISCOURSES

The category of "Academic Discourses" includes public intellectuals and independent scholars as well as university researchers. In terms of media activism, these debates range from media literacy to political economy, media effects research to censorship and propaganda studies. Often these discourses embody divergent views, such as the media literacy debate, where some argue for a "protectionist" position where children are shielded from negative media influence while others argue for media comprehension, where children are taught to think critically about media messages. Similarly, some involved in the media literacy discourse advocate teaching students to "read" media while others argue that students must also be taught how to "write" media. "Writing" media moves beyond textual literacy to include skills for audio, video and web-site production.

Two prominent academic scholars who have contributed to the micro radio debate are Robert McChesney and Mark Crispin Miller. Robert McChesney is an active participant in the ongoing discourse on the political economy of the media. He has written a number of popular press articles in support of micro radio and appears to be in contact with members of the grassroots micro radio community evidenced by the inclusion of his work in two recent books on micro radio and his presence as chairman of the Microradio Empowerment Coalition (MEC). Although McChesney has not published scholarly research on micro radio, he has bridged the gap between the academic discourse of the political economy of the media and the popular press, bringing his intellectual weight to bear on this specific topic.

Miller has taken a similar tact, attempting to bring ideas from the academy into the public forums of the popular press. As mentioned previously in the background section of this research, other scholars who have published academic work on micro radio include Kevin Howley from DePauw University and Ted Coopman from the University of Washington. This brief overview reveals ongoing work within the scholarly community on a host of issues dealing with the media and society. This and other work circulates within the scholarly community and sometimes beyond, when active attempts are made to get academic ideas before a broader audience.

Defining a typology for media activism, these three categories: grassroots organizations (GROs), institutional organizations (NGOs), and academic discourses help in thinking about the types of people and groups involved in this movement and the variety of skills and perspectives brought to bear on this issue. This broad picture of the media activism and reform movement will take on more specific details as we investigate the specific site of micro radio and the actions and discourses picked up and deployed by the many participants. Eyerman and Jamison write,

Social movements develop worldviews that restructure cognition, that re-cognize reality itself. The environmental movement discovered a new territory for social activity which necessitated the development of new scientific theories and methods of investigation. The civil rights movement carved out a new path to self-knowledge and re-cognized American society as fundamentally unjust. (Eyerman & Jamison, 1991, p. 165)

In this case, media activism is re-cognizing the role of media in our democracy. In raising the questions, Who has access?, How is broadcasting organized?, and Why is it the way it is?, media activists are marking a "new territory" for social action and in the process creating a new set of theories and practices about information and technology. The case of micro radio allows for a detailed look at the action of media activists around a specific issue. This deep exploration of one site of media activism reveals the interactions and interconnections of the groups and individuals within the three categories outlined in this proposed typology. In initiating the systematic analysis of a social movement that portends a significant trend in the "information age," this study draws attention to the power and prevalence of this emerging movement as well as contributes to the larger body of social movement research.

NOTE

1. "Examples of memes are tunes, ideas, catch-phrases, clothes fashions, ways of making pots or of building arches. Just as genes propagate themselves in the gene pool by leaping from body to body via sperms or eggs, so memes propagate themselves in the meme pool by

leaping from brain to brain via a process which, in the broad sense, can be called imitation. If a scientist hears or reads about a good idea, he passes it on to his colleagues and students. He mentions it in his articles and his lectures. If the idea catches on, it can be said to propagate itself, spreading from brain to brain." Richard Dawkins, *The Selfish Gene*. Oxford: Oxford University Press, 1989.

2

Activists On-Line: The Micro Radio Network Listserv (MRN) and the Process of Defining a Movement

This chapter is a close examination of communication among micro radio activists. The micro radio issue was a struggle over access to technology that relied on technology as a primary vehicle for advancing the cause. In the last five years, the Internet has emerged as a powerful organizing tool for social movements as well as commercial culture. From the commercial to the political, frivolous to activist newsgroups, listservs, web sites and digital newsletters have all been widely adopted by diverse groups to unite special interests across the globe. Examples of commercial applications of special-interest e-mail communication include daily news digests from the *New York Times*, a daily reminder of the topic of the upcoming episode of "Nightline," an ABC news program, or airfare prices and discounts from travelocity.com. Environmentalists share information through e-mail distribution such as *Rachel's News Weekly* or *Greenwire*, among others. Like the environmental movement, many of the organizations involved in the media activism and reform movement maintain extensive web sites and use e-mail lists to share information.

WHY A LISTSERV?: BACKGROUND AND HISTORY OF THE MRN

Among the hundreds of web sites that address micro radio in particular, one piece of the micro radio communication network has been identified as a major resource for the development and articulation of activist strategy and goals: The MRN. In his essay, "Hardware Handshake: Listserv Forms the Backbone of National Free Radio Movement," Ted Coopman (2000a) documents the primary web site (www.radio4all.org) and listserv (MRN) of the micro radio movement and makes a case for their role in the expansion of micro radio from obscurity in 1995 to a high-profile media policy issue in the year 2000. As an academic researcher and a radio activist, Coopman's work provides insight into the micro radio community and documents many of the significant events throughout the movement history. He was also a frequent contributor to the MRN listserv and as such, his voice played a significant role in shaping the community from within and representing the community to a wider, scholarly audience. He notes that in 1995, while Stephen Dunifer and Free Radio Berkeley were actively engaged in litigation with the FCC, micro radio received little news coverage by the dominant press. By 1998, both the FCC and the NAB had links to either pirate or micro radio on the opening pages of their web sites and news coverage of the issue had risen dramatically (see Chapter 4).

Coopman traced the origin of the MRN back to the establishment of the www.radio4all.org web site in 1996. The web site was said to be a response to the changes taking place at Pacifica Radio. At Pacifica, the national board of directors was making programming and staff changes at KPFA in Berkeley, California, one of the flagship stations of the Pacifica Radio network. These changes were said to be designed to increase audience though many KPFA supporters saw the decisions as attempts to silence progressive community voices at one of the few remaining stations that continued to promote a spirit of public access and community media (Coopman, 1998). As KPFA went through reorganization, ex-Pacifica staff "sought other outlets for their viewpoints" (p. 4). With years of media skills and experience, they began to explore the possibilities offered by low-power radio. Thus, the history of micro radio was intimately connected to other media issues taking place at the same time. The context for the emergence of micro radio is significant to this examination of the discourse that developed among the micro broadcasting community. As we will see, the MRN listserv became a place where voices from the three segments (grassroots, institutional, and academic) of the media activism and reform movement interacted and refined their conceptions of the cognitive territory of micro radio.

Coopman quoted the first post to the MRN listserv in 1998 as a way of establishing the intent of the activists as they expanded the original www.radio4all.org web site into an interactive discussion group. Though the struggle over micro radio was well established by this point with many years of the high-profile Dunifer legal case, hundreds of illegal broadcasters nationwide and aggressive actions by the FCC to shut down those pirates, 1998 was the beginning of the formal legalization process by the FCC. Early 1998 saw formal petitions filed with the FCC calling for the licensing of low-power radio (Coopman, 2000b). By 1999, the FCC would begin accepting public comments on various low-power licensing options. The introduction of the MRN came at a time when more formal interactions between the government and the activist community began to take place. This listserv then proved to be an invaluable tool for refining and deploying the discursive concepts that would dominate the cognitive terrain of this segment of the media activism and reform movement. The initial MRN post stated:

Dear Micro-power Broadcasters and Supporters,
We have created this list specifically for communications to further the micro radio move-

ment, and to support one another in our efforts. The list, it is hoped, will be a tool in assisting with organizing politically, legally, and technically for our mutual defense against the current stepped up campaign of attacks by corporate media and their government allies. (Coopman, 2000a [first MRN post by Lyn Gerry, Sunday, January 4, 1998], p. 4)

The list was established to connect the wide range of people involved in the micro radio debate, sharing information on everything from how to set up a transmitter to how to deal with the FCC when they come knocking. The value of the list as an organizing tool lay in the diversity of knowledge, ideological perspective and skill sets represented on the list. As we will see, this diversity also made for messy discussions at times, with various factions developing and using very strong language to confront (or "flame" in Internet terminology) opponents. Coopman also cited Gerry's statistics on the listserv and the radio4all.org web site, arguing that the listserv increased the use of the resources provided at the web site. By August of 1998, MRN had 119 subscribers with one or two more subscribing weekly (Coopman, 2000a, p. 5). Though this number appears relatively small, as we will see in the next chapter, many of the people subscribed to this list were leaders of micro radio organizations and were the same people quoted in the dominant media news articles and cited by the FCC to support their policy decisions. These were the micro radio broadcasters, organizers of micro radio conferences and demonstrations, authors, and lawyers who moved this issue forward. In many ways, these listserv participants became some the de facto movement leaders who played a significant role in moving media reform discourse from debate within the movement to a wider public audience.

Coopman concluded his analysis of the use of technology by the micro radio activists by placing MRN at the center of an ongoing struggle to increase public access to the radio airwaves.

As the micro radio movement or Free Communication Movement matures and develops, MRN remains the primary forum for the organization and communication for its far-flung members. Information is disseminated, advice is given, and issues are debated that allow this diverse movement to continue to thrive and survive. (Coopman, 2000a, p. 8)

EXPLORING MOVEMENT COSMOLOGY: THE PUBLIC INTEREST AND COMMERCIALISM

Given the history of MRN and the its ongoing role in connecting people interested in the micro radio issue, the historical archive of this e-mail list provided a set of documents that traced the evolution of the micro radio debate from within the movement. The analysis of the micro radio listserv in this chapter is divided into two parts. The first part is an examination of struggles among the listserv subscribers to define the "public interest," a central concept within the micro radio debate in particular and a long-standing concept within FCC broadcast policy in general. Throughout the efforts to promote micro radio, the phrase "the public interest" was used. From Dunifer's legal challenges to web sites to news articles, the concept of the public interest was used to both discredit commercial broadcasters and to describe the benefits of micro radio. The Communication Act of 1934 states that broadcasters must serve "the public interest, convenience and necessity." The concept of the public interest has been shown to be problematic in the past (Streeter, 1996) and the micro radio community encountered many of the historic issues bound up in this discursive concept as they attempt to deploy this idea in the service of micro radio.

The second part of this chapter focuses on the issue of whether LPFM should be commercial on noncommercial. Like the public interest, the issue of commercialism and broadcasting goes all the way back to the earliest government efforts to regulate the electromagnetic spectrum. Media scholars have studied the effects of commercialism on content and up until the Telecommunications Act of 1996, the FCC maintained strict ownership limits on media outlets such as television and radio stations in part out of concern about the effects of consolidated, commercial media. There is a long history of tension between the "public" ownership of the electromagnetic spectrum and the commercial use of that spectrum for private profit and reduced public access to that spectrum. With the media consolidation in the wake of the 1996 Telecom Act, that tension between the public and the private increased and found a release valve in the form of micro radio. Local, low-power radio became an opportunity to protest the public exclusion from the public airwaves and demonstrate what people might do if given the chance to broadcast to their communities. Like the concept of "public interest," the commercialism debate also proved problematic within the micro radio community, demonstrating the difficulty of picking up discursive formations that are heavily encumbered with history and the liberal ideology of the marketplace. Thus these two issues, the public interest and commercialism occupy a central place in the media activism struggle.

The activists' efforts to define these two concepts were part of what Eyerman and Jamison (1991) describe as a process of developing a movement cosmology or worldview. Though many of the ideas around media activism have been discussed and debated for many years as communication technology has continued to develop and proliferate, there have not been many focused issues or events that have helped the movement to coalesce and publicly display its knowledge and new appropriations and definitions of terms and concepts. Micro radio provided a tangible, local issue to demonstrate concepts such as localism and public access by example rather than abstract theory. Micro radio provided the opportunity for the specialized knowledge developed by media activists to attain a publicly recognizable form. In addition to demonstrating independent, local media-making by broadcasting illegally, the activists had to work out the discursive arguments that would be deployed against opponents to LPFM. The process of working out these arguments involved exploring the assumptions that make up the "emancipatory aims" of the movement. In describing the work of the environmental movement, Eyerman and Jamison write, "The movement created the cosmology, the worldview that, in turn, formed the assumptions through which new thoughts were thought in a variety of disciplines and areas of knowledge" (Eyerman & Jamison, 1991, p. 73). The following sections document micro radio activists struggling to define their worldview, working to establish an effective discourse upon which to promote their agenda.

WORKING THROUGH THE ISSUES: ACTIVISTS STRUGGLE TO DEFINE "PUBLIC INTEREST"

In this section, examines how the micro radio activists who participated in the MRN listserv struggled to define a key concept: the "public interest." The MRN list contained a multiplicity of issues and articulations worthy of attention and analysis, though the concept of the public interest and in the next section, the issue of commercialism, warrant attention for a number of reasons. First, the concept of the "public interest," is woven throughout the history of FCC policy. Similarly, the term public interest appears throughout the legal arguments developed by the National Lawyers Guild Committee for Democratic Communication (NLGCDC) in the defense of Black Liberation Radio and Free Radio Berkeley. Given the central place this term occupies in the discourse around micro radio, examining the way the activists struggled to define the term among themselves reveals some of the priorities of this movement and the process of movement formation as the three types of social movement participants (grassroots, institutional and academic) worked together to find common ground.

The second recurring debate on this listserv that embodied many of the issues micro radio attempted to address was the question of whether LPFM should be commercial or noncommercial. The question of the relationship between advertising and media content has been the focus of many communication scholars. As micro radio advocates attempted to gain the "freedom" to access the airwaves, the movement was divided about whether that included the freedom to fund the small stations as the local broadcasters saw fit, or if noncommercial status must be enforced across the boards out of fear of replicating the dominant commercial media model on a smaller scale. As we will see, these two discursive struggles were overlapping and woven together in many ways.

Within the first month of the creation of the MRN listserv (from now on referred to as MRN), the issue of the "public interest" was raised and debated. This initial thread reveals the difficulty in defining this concept and the variety of perspectives brought to bear on this policy term.[1] On January 15, 1998, Steve Provizer of Free Radio Allston posted a message titled, "Public Interest." Free Radio Allston was an illegal micro station in the metro-Boston area that has received a letter of commendation from the Boston City Council for its contribution to local community affairs programming. In his message about the public interest, Provizer wrote:

We talk a lot about it, but can we agree on what it is? The NAB has. They say public interest means 'giving the public what it wants.' . . . I believe that if the cause of access to the radio dial is to be taken up by more than a small group of people, we have to define what this phrase means. . . . We have to show our communities that issues which are really important to them are not being dealt with, or are being dealt with from a limited, biased perspective. (MRN post by Stephen Provizer, January 15, 1998)

Provizer's challenge sparked an extended discussion about what concepts should be invoked in the pursuit of micro radio. As a participant on MRN and someone involved in a micro station, Provizer was an individual acting within a grassroots organization, taking part in the micro radio site of the media activist and reform movement. As we will see from the MRN, there was not a uniform pursuit of micro radio. While some people wanted to see micro radio legalized and regulated, others argued for the open use of the airwaves with the FCC acting as arbiter when interference occurred. These different goals necessitated different discourses. The public interest could be used as a concept to speak the language of regulation *to* a government body or could imply the regulation *by* a government body that had not proven itself to be acting in the public interest. Provizer went on to list four areas he would include in any definition of public interest programming.

1. Coverage and discussion of political events on the local, city, national, and international level, including access for "alternative" politics.
2. Access to program time for local art and civic groups to discuss concerts, exhibitions, zoning, traffic, and other issues.
3. Multi-language programming.
4. "Public Access" radio frequencies. (MRN post by Stephen Provizer, January 15, 1998)

Provizer qualified number four, adding that public participation in media production had a number of secondary effects that translate into involvement in a host of community issues. Adding one final thought, Provizer thought the concept of the public interest should be used as a tool to challenge the renewal of broadcast licenses, arguing that many corporate commercial radio stations are not serving the public interest as he had defined it.

This initial post was followed by a response from Ted Coopman, a self-described "rogue" scholar who had researched the micro radio issue, presented his work at academic conferences, and published articles on the subject in peer reviewed journals. As a scholar working on this issue, Coopman was someone who connected the academic discourses to the grassroots individuals and organizations. His post exemplified this type of connection, beginning with "A good point of attack on commercial media is the effect of monopolization and consolidation of local programming. Bagdikian's 'The Media Monopoly' is a good primer for this" (MRN Post by Ted Coopman, January 15, 1998). Thus Coopman attempted to expand the discussion with a reference to critical academic scholarship. It is interesting how quickly the issue of the public interest became entangled with other issues of media critique. Coopman continued,

Locality, or the lack of, is a fairly hot concern in many areas of media. The FCC has "must carry" rules for local cable providers that require that they dedicate a certain percentage of channels to local TV stations. . . . I believe that locality is a chink in the armor of the NAB. They would be hard pressed to defend it in terms of radio. Also, if the FCC was so concerned about it for cable, why are they not concerned about radio? (MRN Post by Ted Coopman, January 15, 1998)

Coopman used the term locality, often referred to as localism, a concept described in detail in Chapter 3. The apparent argument Coopman made was that the dominant commercial radio broadcasters were not serving the public interest because of the lack of localism in their programming. The FCC was thought to be committed to localism as evidenced by the "must carry" rules applied to cable TV system owners. Drawing on the FCC's policy history, Coopman argued that localism and the public interest are intimately connected.

Micheal Eisenmenger posted the third message in this thread. His signature file indicated he was involved with Paper Tiger Television and the domain of his e-mail address (rutgers.edu) indicated he was involved with Rutgers University. Paper Tiger is an organization that creates and distributes independent media. It is a grassroots organization, relying on many hours of volunteer time and actively connecting individuals with the tools and knowledge to make media products. At the same time, they have been involved in activist media production for almost twenty years, making them an institution among independent media producers and distributors. In this sense, Paper Tiger straddles the space between grassroots organization and institution in the typology of media activism. Eisenmenger himself appears to occupy space within the academic world as well, thus connecting the three segments of this movement typology. Eisenmenger wrote,

Having a position paper or media kit that clarifies or redefines the "public interest" could only help the micro radio movement in its attempts to legitimize itself under the gaze (or glaze) of public opinion. In other words, take the high ground, it's wide open, especially since the commercial broadcasting corporations aren't exactly clammering to get there. (MRN post by Micheal Eisenmenger, January 16, 1998)

Without defining "public interest," Eisenmenger advocated the movement use the concept to take some form of moral (or public opinion) high ground. Although the public interest was not clearly defined, it was clear to Eisenmenger that commercial broadcasting was not serving it. His post continued with plans for challenging the commercial broadcasters:

Here in the U.S., the FCC's ill-defined and minimal public interest requirements were nearly gutted under Reagan—along with the fairness doctrine. It seems commercial broadcasters in the U.S. now operate under few restrictions. Nonetheless, I think it could be worthwhile to challenge license renewals, if only for the sake of pointing out the disparity between more authentic forms of broadcasting. Here in NYC, the right-wing AM talk radio station WABC is up for renewal this spring. It may be worthwhile to direct some energy that way during the public comment period. (MRN post by Micheal Eisenmenger, January 16, 1998)

Although he critiqued the "ill-defined" public interest standards of the FCC, Eisenmenger advocated the continued use of this undefined concept to attack "right-wing" commercial broadcasters he deemed inappropriate. Thus without explicit definition, the public interest was invoked as a tool to limit speech on the airwaves at the same time that it is being used as an argument for the expansion of diverse, local content. This hypocrisy was quickly noted in the following post to MRN.

Jesse Walker is an media historian and author. He is a self-described "anarchist libertarian" who pulls no punches in his postings to the MRN. His comments regarding the public interest were true to form:

Since "public interest" regulations (a) have been, from the beginning, used to crush interesting and dissident radio, (b) violate the First Amendment, and (c) are not particularly popular with the public, I would *not* advise basing anyone's case against media monopoly around them. (MRN post from Jesse Walker, January 16, 1998)

Walker made the case that public interest regulations have been used to limit free speech, not expand it. Walker pointed out the complex and dubious nature of the "public interest" as a discursive tool for promoting micro radio. His experience researching the history of broadcast regulation informed his position and thus we see another academic perspective injected into the debate, encouraging activists to be careful about what discourses they deploy. Walker made the point that historical baggage attached to concepts can limit their effectiveness. What may appear to be a guardian of the public may in fact turn out to have a history of limiting public speech. This type of conceptual and linguistic history was important for media activists to understand if new meanings for concepts such as the public interest were ever to be established. This level of exchange demonstrates the contributions made by various people who occupy different spaces with the media activism typology.

After his words of caution about the use of the public interest, Walker took on Eisenmenger's call to attack right-wing AM radio. Walker wrote,

I especially would not try to go after a right-wing AM station's license; that only puts you in the camp of the censors, as well as in the paradoxical position of attacking a station that *is* doing public-interest programming, albeit public-interest programming you disagree with. (MRN post from Jesse Walker, January 16, 1998)

Walker inverted a popular conception (e.g., attack right-wing talk radio because there is too much of it) and redefined the public interest to include the freedom to broadcast right-wing ideas without government interference. Walker concluded his post with,

I *do* think it's worth arguing that micro radio allows people to do the kind of public-interest programming the corporate stations often ignore, and that it does so without relying on the heavy hand of federal regulation. That's the kind of argument that might appeal to folks who don't automatically side with hippies and black nationalists who get into fights with the federal government. (MRN post from Jessie Walker, January 16, 1998)

Walker turned the debate from an attempt to define the pubic interest into a broad defense of public participation and access to media through micro radio. His reference to "black nationalists" and "hippies" was a reference to Mbanna Kantako, the founder of Black Liberation Radio, and Stephen Dunifer, the founder of Free Radio Berkeley. Walker attempted to move the debate out of the realm of traditional "left" politics and in the process make the arguments for micro radio more appealing to a broader political spectrum. This move away from one ideological perspective is a classic example of the new social movement model, where movements are said to be more goal focused (advancing micro radio) and less attached to adhering to a single ideological principle. As we will see, Walker brought a contrary perspective to many debates on the MRN, always provoking a response and usually redirecting the debate.

Following Walker's post, the discussion of how to define and appropriate the term public interest took a turn back toward the question of localism. Crash Knorr began his/her (their?) post by responding to Eisenmenger. "At least you are honest about wanting to silence those who disagree with you" (MRN post by Crash Knorr, January 16, 1998). This was again another check within the community, making sure that in the quest for democratic media, repressive tactics are not employed. Knorr also addressed localism when he wrote:

To me, one of the main issues is local origination. Locally originated programming is more interesting (and more endangered in the current regulatory climate) than satellite feeds, syndicated shows, or the playing of recorded music that is churned out by distant media conglomerates. Local origination means giving more people a voice, and protecting local culture from the onslaught of multinational corporate culture. (MRN post by Crash Knorr, January 16, 1998)

This argument followed Walker's proposition for the inclusion of more voices, not the exclusion of those you disagree with. Although Walker jumped to the defense of right-wing radio, no one argued in defense of "distant media conglomerates" though they too may well be serving a segment of the public interest. What began to emerge in this debate was a wide ideological space reserved for individuals, with corporate entities bearing the brunt of the criticism for the lack of "public interest."

A final post to this thread offers a nice bridge to our next section on the question of commercialism. After this flurry of posts about the public interest in the winter of 1998, Coopman weighed in again calling for a reconsideration of the larger goals of micro radio.

Maybe before we start flinging regulatory suggestions around, we should discuss what we want micro radio to be, what we think it should be, and what it can do for us the people it serves. This might help us to decide issues such as commercial vs. non-commercial, local origination, and single vs. multi-station ownership. (MRN post by Ted Coopman, February 19, 1998)

Thus a discussion that began as an attempt to define a discursive tool (the public interest) to advance micro radio turned into a larger examination of the goals of micro radio activists in general. Coopman's post reflected his desire to come to some sort of agreement about these issues in spite of the heterogeneous nature of the movement. These posts to MRN show the activists struggling to develop a coherent set of concepts to promote local, democratic media and the difficulty inherent in creating an open media system that was not open to commercial consolidation. Coopman articulated this when he continued:

For me, the biggest concerns are to avoid the absorption of mass quantities of micro radio licenses by commercial or religious networks and the re-broadcasting of networked programming at the expense of local programming. . . .

If big business smells money in micro radio, it will be swallowed whole. Will micro radio be just another way to make money?

It is supposed to be a way (I contend) for those without power and money to have a voice.

What is the best way to serve that? A way to protect micro radio without strangling it? (MRN post by Ted Coopman, February 19, 1998)

Coopman raised issues that continued to plague the micro radio community: how to finance local radio and how to encourage all voices including religious ones without becoming another commercial network. At this point, the thread of "the public interest" had expanded into a host of issues that centered on questions of money, advertising and commercialism.

MOVEMENT INTELLECTUALS

Before continuing the examination of the MRN debate about commercialism, it is important to think about what took place on the listserv and the role of individuals in the development of the cognitive terrain of a movement. The divergent and heated debate among a select group of people on the MRN was indicative of Eyerman and Jamison's (1991) conception of the role of intellectuals within social movement. Eyerman and Jamison argue that the role of "movement intellectuals" is critical in the development of a movement and that the role evolves as the movement develops.

All activists in social movements are, in some sense, "movement intellectuals," because through their activism they contribute to the formation of the movement's collective identity, to making the movement what it is. (Eyerman & Jamison, 1991, p. 94)

Thus Walker, Coopman and others consistently contribute to the MRN debate while other people were out broadcasting or taking part in other areas of movement praxis. By examining the MRN debates, this study does not seek to categorize individuals but rather to follow the process of development that resulted in an FCC decision to reverse policy and license LPFM. By viewing the MRN debate as a site where the cognitive terrain of the movement was debated and explored among movement intellectuals, this project continues the research of Eyerman and Jamison (1991) that placed the movement intellectuals at the service of the movement and not the other way around. "We can say that we reverse the direction in the Leninist models; for us it is movements, as cognitive praxis, that lead and direct intellectuals rather than intellectuals that lead and direct movements" (Eyerman & Jamison, 1991, p. 99). The MRN provided the opportunity to examine the intimate conversation among micro radio advocates as they built their movement. The process of on-line debate revealed pieces of the content and character of the movement regardless of whether a clear resolution or consensus was ever achieved. The process of communicating about micro radio issues on-line proved to be a tangible site to witness the "societal formation of intellectual activity" (Eyerman & Jamison, 1991, p. 98). If media activism is in fact a social movement where new knowledge is being generated about the relationship between media and democracy, the process whereby this knowledge is worked out becomes a valuable site for research. The MRN provided one set of historical documents that gave a glimpse into the micro radio activists' exploration of the cognitive terrain, a terrain that included the relationship between communication technology and the process of democracy.

COMMERCIAL VERSUS NONCOMMERCIAL?

The question of whether micro radio stations can or should allow commercials on their broadcasts weaved in and out of the discussion on the MRN, recurring in a number of instances. The initial discussion of the place of commercialism within micro radio emerged from a thread titled, "regulatory fervor," where ideas about how to regulate micro radio were proposed and discussed. Some of this debate took place during the preceding debate about the public interest. The coterminous nature of these debates reveals the connections between these issues and the efforts of this community of activists to work through the problems involved in establishing new, publicly accessible media technology.

Coopman proposed a seven-point plan to guide the implementation of micro radio. This proposal prompted a heated discussion about who would enforce the regulations and the potential of increasing state interference in local radio. The fourth point initiated a thread about commercialism:

4. Funding: Advertising should be modeled after public stations. Underwriting and sponsorship of programming blocks by persons/organizations/businesses that operate or serve the stations community. No Commercials. (MRN post by Ted Coopman, February 17, 1998)

Walker was one of the first to respond to this post, noting how some micro station operators chose to include commercials.

Free Radio 1055, among others, sells ads to local businesses that can't afford time on the area's giant, absentee-owned outlets. Bill thinks this is a valid use of his station, and so do I. And yes, I hate listening to commercials too, but I'm not in charge of 1055. Do you really want to ban this? (MRN post by Jesse Walker, February 17, 1998)

A distaste and distrust of advertising was a common theme among the political left. Given that the micro radio movement was reacting in large part to the impact of commercial broadcasting, a desire to limit commercial influences was understandable. Walker wanted to reconsider this assumption while he raised questions about the impact of a central authority determining the shape of local media. Thus two ideas that were central to the micro radio movement created a discursive struggle. On one hand, micro radio was about local communities determining their own news and cultural content as they saw fit. On the other hand, micro radio was responding to the effect of consolidated commercial media and many of the activists in turn were hoping to prevent the commercial consolidation of micro radio. Coopman responded to Walker with:

I guess I was looking at it as activist vs. commercial stations. Many of the stations I am familiar with would never run a commercial because they don't want to be like the commercial stations. Is this a social movement or an opportunity for entrepenures (or both!?)?

There is that idealism that we could make it something different, but if you force a particular way on people, is that the real sell out (not commercials)?

I stand corrected. I agree, the less rules the better. (MRN post by Ted Coopman, February 17, 1998)

This exchange depicts the tension between the aspiration of many of the activists who saw micro radio as a tool for social change and other activists who wanted local access to radio technology and were willing to let each locale determine the shape of that broadcasting. Centralized authority became the demon in these posts. The presence of commercials was secondary to the question of who determined whether or not there were commercials.

As a broadcaster with Radio Free Allston (RFA), Stephen Provizer responded to the tensions raised by arguing for limits on commercials on micro radio.

There was always an active debate at RFA about whether commercials from local merchants was a good idea. There are lots of things that bear on this, but I think the two underlying questions are: What do you think the station stands for and Who do you want the station to serve? . . .

If a station doesn't make itself available to address all conflicting political and commercial concerns (money is especially important to people who don't have it), then I don't believe that station can claim it represents the "community" as opposed to being just another "vested interest." (MRM post by Stephen Provizer, February 17, 1998)

Provizer acknowledged the complexity of codifying micro radio regulations and argued for the local resolution of this issue. Limiting the financial options for running a micro station would effect the shape and scope of the programming that station could offer. This question of "community representation" raised additional questions about community sponsors. Do multinational corporations with a local presence (i.e., Walmart) qualify as a community business? These issues had no clear resolution and people such as Provizer advocated the decentralized model of regulation, allowing different stations to reach different conclusions according to their need.

The MRN thread on commercialism evolved into a series of proposals and speculation about designating certain frequencies nationwide for micro radio and a number of other technical issues related to spectrum allocation. The crux of the commercialism discourse reemerged in full bloom six months later under the subject heading "commercialism." This disscussion continued to reveal the diverse, dynamic nature of the micro radio activists as they attempted to define the cognitive space that micro radio occupied. With input from a variety of perspectives within the activist typology, the discourse moved in unpredictable directions, ultimately yielding a more complex and nuanced analysis of the issues involved in establishing broadcast policy.

Pete triDish, a founding member of the Prometheus Radio Project and an active member of the micro radio community, revived the discussion about commercialism in a post titled, "Mickey Mouse Microradio?" TriDish (whose e-mail signature file reads, "a short, cylindrical, transparent piece of laboratory glassware, useful in observing resistant strains of culture in liquid media") posted a draft of an article about commercialism in micro radio to the MRN. This article summarized many of the points that had been argued regarding the pros and cons of advertising on micro radio. TriDish noted some of the potential benefits of allowing small businesses to advertise on micro stations.

Hippolito Cuevas's station in Connecticut—a station that was very quickly accepted by the Latino community in a town where a fourth of the population is Latino and there is no Spanish language radio. Cuevas makes the argument that there would be no way for him to make his radio station work without some commercial revenues. He says that the commercials that he would take—for example, from local stores that could never afford the outrageous rates of regular stations—are in fact a form of community service. (MRN post by Pete triDish, May 9, 1998)

The micro radio community was faced with the tension between the financial necessity of running community radio and the potential for that radio to become just another part of the dominant commercial network. Although he acknowledged the problems identified by Cuevas, triDish ended up arguing for noncommercial status for micro radio.

I am deeply concerned that due to the predatory nature of the corporate behemoths of our age, any micro-radio proposal that allows for any type of commercialism will be doomed to being swallowed up by big business. . . . It betrays the promise and potential of micro radio as a tool for local self expression to make it just another billboard for the shrieking salesmen that already have too many invasive venues to hawk their wares. (MRN post by Pete triDish, May 9, 1998)

As was the case throughout this discourse, "local self-expression" apparently did not include the right to advertise. This exchange traversed a terrain that academics have spent a great deal of time studying: the effect of advertising on content. The free, diverse, alternative values assigned to micro radio by many of its proponents were fiercely defended from "advertising" and the idea that *any* commercial presence would limit or corrupt the content of micro radio. The defense of "free" radio brought with it a set of ideas that limited freedom and contained the seed for the recreation of a new system of bureaucratic regulation. The question became, how free could free communications be if commercial communication was outlawed? Was one set of bureaucratic structures being proposed to replace another?

Crash Knorr responded positively to triDish with a vehement attack on commercialism, invoking a vision of a permanent, undeniable bond between advertising and content.

Commercialism or NPR-style underwriting must be avoided in micro broadcasting. If money is one of the motivating factors in a communication medium, you cannot trust *any* of the information coming from it. Commerce poisons everything it touches. (MRN post by Crash Knorr, May 10, 1998)

Knorr's sentiment was supported by Peter Franck, a lawyer with the National Lawyers Guild Committee on Democratic Communication and one of the lawyers who worked on the defense of Mbanna Kantako and Stephen Dunifer. Franck wrote:

As far as I can see, there is no difference between advertising on "commercial" stations and "underwriting" on so called public stations. Actually, industry mags consistently point out that "underwriting" on public stations is far cheaper, per listener reached, per minute, per whatever, than advertising on commercial stations, i.e. the "public" system is being sold out cheaply.

As far as I'm personally concerned, non-commercial means nobody gets to pay for having anything specific go out on the air. No "I give you X $$ and you broadcast Y message or X program." It's the camel's nose under the tent of free speech. (MRN post by Peter Franck, May 11, 1998)

Both Knorr and Franck argued for a noncommercial micro radio system as a way to prevent the influence of money, big business, or even small business from influencing content. One question that remained unanswered was the effect on content of a lack of money and reliance on volunteer staff. The limitations presented by underfunding were never discussed. Disregarding the issue of station funding, the National Lawyers Guild eventually supported a noncommercial LPFM model and the FCC would cite the guild's comments repeatedly in their *Report and Order*. Instead of continuing to explore questions about station funding, the MRN debate was steered back toward issues of local control and free speech.

Walker entered this discussion with a similar argument to the one he had used in February. Walker began his post with the idea that advertising was overt and identifiable whereas underwriting was less transparent, making it more difficult to identify potential conflicts of interest. He also cited a bit of history, noting that "Even in the amateur broadcasting days of the 1910s, when the medium was dominated by hobbyists, some stations ran ads" (MRN post by Jessie Walker, May 11,

1998). Reiterating his argument for local control on the issue of commercials, Walker wrote,

Look: I don't like listening to most ads, but that's my business (as it were). If you don't want commercials on your micro station, don't put them there. The decision should be yours, not an FCC bureaucrat's. (MRN post by Jessie Walker, May 11, 1998)

Choosing to ignore larger questions about the possibilities of commercial influence on content, Walker remained committed to the autonomy of the individual station. This drew a sharp response from Steve O., another listserv participant:

Even if commercials aren't the same as underwriting, the process is essentially the same. There's no point in running a thirty second spot for a for-profit corporation unless you are being paid some sort of funding to air such insults to public intelligence.

What happens is that money becomes taken for granted and when the station is fully dependent on that money, it has to do as the advertiser wants or the plug is pulled. That's basic capitalism. I haven't even read Manufacturing Consent by Herman and Chomsky, and I can tell you that. (MRN post by Steve O., May 11, 1998)

This argument is closer to a political economy position. Steve did not argue that advertisers effect message content directly necessarily, rather, the station would become dependent on advertising dollars for its operating expenses and this would have an impact on content. It is interesting that the academic arguments of Herman and Chomsky are cited yet academic research that challenges negative assumptions about advertising was neglected. This points to a selective use of academic discourses by some in their construction of the micro radio discourse.

Walker responded with an argument about the relationship between advertising and free speech: "A commercial *is* speech. If you think it shouldn't be protected by the First Amendment, that's fine, but then don't present yourself as a defender of free speech" (MRN Post by Jessie Walker, May 12, 1998). Walker again raised the question: How do you argue for a policy to allow micro radio based on free speech if the policies you want to implement do not allow free speech? He failed to cite the legal distinctions between commercial and political speech, though he repeatedly challenged the group to think about the effects of limiting one type of speech while attempting to promote another. Walker also injected a more sophisticated conception of the advertiser/audience relationship in his response to Steve O.'s depiction of "insults to the public intelligence":

Don't assume everyone listening to a commercial is a passive consumer. Lots of people talk back to ads, including non-ideologues who wouldn't know socialism if it moved in next door. (MRN post by Jesse Walker, May 12, 1998)

Although Walker does not cite sources, the idea of an active audience comes directly out of academic discourses, particularly cultural studies. Scholars have realized that consumers are productive in that they produce meaning from the material and cultural texts they consume.

As the issue of commercialism was connected to free speech issues, the discourse took a turn back into regulatory policy. In cautioning against too much reliance on free speech issues, Coopman reminded the group that FCC regulation of broadcasting has consistently been up held in the courts. Unlike printing or the Internet, broadcasting is limited by the availability of electromagnetic spectrum, thus the issue of spectrum scarcity is at the foundation of the FCC's regulatory authority and the incumbent limits on free speech that come with that regulation. Coopman wrote,

As far as deciding what is free speech and what is not, I urge people to think who would make those calls and how you would feel if you were on the pointy end of them. You may think commercials are "different" and not worthy of protection, but remember, there are many who think the same about YOUR favorite topic or cause. (MRN post by Ted Coopman, May 12, 1998)

This fair-minded approach was responded to by Stephen Dunifer, the founder of Free Radio Berkeley, seen by many as a leader of the micro radio movement because of his high profile legal battles with the FCC. Dunifer wrote,

Corporations are a legal fiction and do not have rights, just privilege—despite the Santa Clara decision. Commercial influence of any sort has absolutely no place in community radio or micropower broadcasting. Anyone who supports allowing commercials and such should just go out and apply for a commercial broadcast license. To hell with corporations and their supposed "free speech" rights. (MRN post by Stephen Dunifer, May 12, 1998)

Coming from a central figure in the movement, this emphatic opposition to *any* commercial presence on micro radio drew immediate support and criticism. Howard, whose signature file identifies him with Free Radio Gainsville responded, "Right on Stephen, I'm in your camp. Corporations are legal entities with no inherent rights, including free speech" (MRN post by Howard, May 12, 1998). Howard's reference to "camp" was a reminder of the divisions within the movement and on the MRN listserv. The on-line discourse was one place where those divisions manifest themselves, providing a space for the articulation of specific ideological and political loci. These divisions appeared fluid as the discourse evolved and progressed.

Walker was the first to challenge Dunifer's vehement opposition to commercialism. In his response titled, "Who Has Rights?," Walker used humor and satire to critique Dunifer's argument.

Since this engages absolutely none of the arguments that I and others have raised (and ignores the difference between "allowing" commercials and wanting to put them on one's own station . . .) it's pointless to argue back. I will, however, present three cognate arguments:

1. DJs do not have rights, just privileges. Musical influence of any sort has absolutely no place in community radio or micropower broadcasting. Anyone who supports allowing compact discs and such should just go out and apply for a commercial broadcast license. To hell with the DJs and their supposed "free speech" rights (MRN post by Jessie Walker, May 12, 1998)

Walker continued his post with more satirical examples of groups that "do not have rights." His second example substituted "anarchist" for DJ and followed the wording of the above paragraph very closely. His third example used "Jews" as the foil. These examples appeared to be quite pointed, given that many in the micro community believe in the sanctity of the DJ, glorify anarchism and respect the rights of minority religions. Walker immediately followed this post with a response to Howard. Referring to Howard's assertion that corporations were legal entities with no free speech rights, Walker wrote:

Since I oppose incorporation, I oppose corporations, and thus on a certain level I agree with this. But it's utterly irrelevant to the issue of free speech and commercialism. Consider:

Do members of corporations have free speech?

Do "legal entities" such as unions, political pressure groups, and unincorporated businesses have free speech?

Do micro broadcasters have free speech? If so, can't *they* run an ad, even if it's the product of a corporation?

And just *who* is it that is going to enforce your rules against commercial speech? The Anarchist Police?(MRN post by Jesse Walker, May 12, 1998)

Walker continued to hammer home the idea that limiting the speech of one group opened up the potential to limit speech for everyone, a foundational argument throughout the history of the defense of free speech in this country. Walker's two posts, with their combination of satire and rational questions, prompted a vehement response from Stephen Dunifer.

Dunifer responded to Walker with a message titled, "Hey Jesse! Go Fuck Yourself." The body of this message read, "Take your corporate suck-up love for commercialism somewhere else" (MRN post by Stephen Dunifer, May 12, 1998). Thus a discourse about free speech devolved into a first hand attempt to silence a member of the micro radio community. Dunifer's post drew a variety of responses from a range MRN members. Responding to Dunifer's hostile tone, Bill G. wrote:

Jeez Steve, You sound like someone who just lost an argument and knows it. "Go fuck yourself" isn't a very productive response. For my two cents, Jesse's comments are welcome. (MRN post by Bill G. [blive], May 13, 1998)

This support for Walker and "productive" communication prompted this response from Bob Marston, who wrote:

Mr. Walker's thoughts as expressed on this list are TOTALLY DEVOID OF ANY KIND OF POWER ANALYSIS.

Like every Libertarian he starts his arguments talking about personal rights and redirects the conversation to the supreme right, the right to make money. (MRN post by Bob Marston, May 13, 1998)

Bill G. responded to Marston with:

I think there is certainly enough hypocrisy being exhibited when a micro radio discussion resorts to commentary such as "Go fuck yourself. Take your thoughts somewhere else." The libertarian point of view might not be YOUR point of view, but isn't micro radio supposed to be about the exchange of ideas? (MRN post by Bill G. [blive], May 13, 1998)

Another MRN participant, John (e-mail name Phlegm) responded to Dunifer with a sharp critique of the idea of limiting debate on the MRN:

Yes, yes, yes. This is the kind of attitude I like to see out of the de facto figurehead for the microbroadcasting movement. No room for dissent, no hope for compromise. . . . Let ten thousand transmitters spewing the same neo-hippie social activism bloom! So much for that "accessibility" thing people always bring up when it comes to legal LPFM. (MRN post by John [Phlegm], May 13, 1998)

John reframed Dunifer's own slogan, "let 10,000 transmitters bloom" to reflect the absolutist position Dunifer called for in his attack on Walker. John continued his post with:

While I will tolerate the professional social activists springing up on my local dial, because they're trying to get a message across, I'll also tolerate the guy who programs eclecticism while throwing in a couple of ads for the local record store or coffeehouse so he can make the electric bill and keep the station on the air. . . . My dream has always been to run my own station . . . and I want to do it my way. Brace yourself: I'll even probably take a couple of national media buys, too, just so I can make fun of the spots after they play;). (MRN post by John [Phlegm], May 13, 1998)

John raised the idea of critiquing commercials or recontextualizing them on the air as a way to disempower them. This was another example of the power of appropriation, where individuals make their own meaning out of advertising texts, in this case a resistant meaning. As a closing point (albeit a somewhat arbitrary one given the continuous nature of listserv communication), Walker attempted to answer his critics and restate his position:

My interest in radio has nothing to do with an interest in making money. Indeed, I think radio is being destroyed by people more interested in money than in the medium. The difference between you and me is, I don't think it's the desire to make money that's destroying radio; I think it's (among other things) several decades of public policy that's given more power to the corporate drones and less to the radio craftsmen and artists. (MRN post by Jesse Walker, May 13, 1998)

This piece of a rather extended post reveals Walker's attempt to define the debate as he saw it and make sure people debated his *ideas*, not the politics of libertarianism or other ideologies. He attempted to respond to the arguments, not the accusations, though he too resorted to personal attacks in closing his post, directing his final comment to Dunifier. "If you really think my comments reflect a 'corporate suck-up love for commercials,' I suggest you reread them when you aren't stoned" (MRN post by Jesse Walker, May 13, 1998). And thus the discourse continued and evolved in a variety of forms, recurring a number of times in the two years since this initial heated exchange.

SO MANY E-MAILS, SO MANY IDEAS

Phew, after wading through an extended summary of two issues debated on the MRN listserv, it is easy to come away entertained though wondering, so what? In looking over the shape and form of the struggle to pick up and redefine discourses of "public interest" and "commercialism," three significant themes emerge. First, the MRN discussion provided an intimate, detailed picture of a group of activists working through the process of establishing the goals and core principles around micro radio, mapping the cognitive terrain of micro radio if you will. This listserv exchange is a snapshot of the material ways in which discourses are said to structure social life. Picking up discursive formations with extensive historical baggage required serious work to redefine and work through the limitations and possibilities associated with this terminology. Second, the MRN discourse revealed the power of individuals, movement intellectuals, within a social movement. Though the listserv had between 120 and 200 subscribers, only a few individuals engaged the debates and offered their opinions. Finally, the MRN discourse included the active participation of individuals from the three categories (grassroots, institutions, academics) of the media activism typology.

One example of how the micro radio activists came to a limited consensus on these and other issues was chronicles by Ted Coopman (2000b). As an active member of the listserv and the micro radio community at large, Coopman described the development of a *Joint Statement on Micro Radio* that detailed the points of agreement within the community and allowed groups and individuals to join in a common statement of vision that would then be submitted to the FCC. The development of this statement was a difficult process given the divisions within the movement. Coopman divided the activists into two main camps, the non-commercial advocates led by the Microradio Empowerment Coalition and the "commies," or those willing to settle for some limited commercial micro stations, led by the Amherst Alliance.

The Microadio Empowerment Coalition was formed around several activist organizations; Project Censored, FAIR (Fairness and Accuracy in Reporting), CDC (National Lawyers Guild Committee on Democratic Communication), Radio4all, and chaired by academic Robert McChesney . . . Amherst was formed around Nickolaus Leggett, Judith Leggett, and Don Schellhardt [the authors of one of the original 1998 petitions to the FCC to license LPFM]. Amherst was very well organized and had made contact with many emerging low power radio groups such as Americans For Radio Diversity and REC Networks. (Coopman, 2000b, p. 6)

Coopman attempted to bring the two factions together by focusing on the core issues that both sides could agree on.

I became convinced that there had to be some sort of document everyone could sign. This way, we could drive home the central important issues to the FCC and show them and our opposition that we, as a movement, were capable of unified action. It became apparent that the central issues of technical requirements and ownership restrictions were key to creating a functional community based low power service. (Coopman, 2000b, p. 6)

Coopman believed that a joint statement could cover a few core issues and that other opinions could be filed individually, thus harnessing the power of collective voice while encouraging diversity within the movement.

Coopman's *Joint Statement on Microradio* ended up avoiding the issue of commercialism and focused instead on ownership limits and other technical issues. Before the statement was submitted to the FCC on August 2, 1999, thirty organizations, including MEC, Amherst, and the CDC had signed on, as well as 101 individuals from seventeen states, all coordinated over three weeks primarily on-line (p. 8). The divisive issues of commercialism and amnesty for pirates were left for each group to resolve. Given the diverse, decentralized nature of this movement, real consensus would be hard to imagine. Through the MRN, issues were debated a range of positions established. This open debate allowed groups and individuals to form their own opinions and comment to the FCC as they saw fit. This heterogeneity was a by-product of a leaderless, grassroots movement. Efforts such as Coopman's joint statement were an indication of the groups' ability to find common ground while agreeing to disagree on the rest. Social movements are messy, chaotic, explorations that require a wide range of ideas and approaches and the MRN provided a glimpse of the movement as it ventured into the uncharted waters of micro radio broadcast policy.

NOTE

1. A thread is a series of messages responding to the same subject. On e-mail lists and newsgroups, threads often start with the same subject heading, though long threads will often branch out into a number of specific issues with individuals responding to pieces of the larger discussion.

3

Public Radio and Christians: Micro Radio Activists Struggle to Define "the Other"

With any social movement, the opposition must be identified and confronted if the social problem is to be altered or resolved. In the case of micro radio, two groups occupied complex and unexpected positions. National Public Radio (NPR) and the Christian broadcasting community played active roles in the struggle over micro radio, though their positions were not always consistent and the activist communities' response to these two groups required considerable debate. The three years of listserv discussion (1998–2000) revealed numerous threads addressing NPR and Christian broadcasters. The ongoing presence of these groups within the micro radio debate was an indication of both their influence on this issue and the complexity of the relationship between the various players.

Scholars have argued that a primary component of the formative stage of a social movement includes the identification of the Other (Touraine, 1981; Eyerman & Jamison, 1991). The Other is said to be more than an "intellectual construction," and often includes individual "social actors" and "institutions" who must be engaged in a strategic manner (Eyerman & Jamison, 1991, pp. 101–102). Initially, micro radio activists identified the FCC as the primary Other, as they were the ones who set the policies that eliminated LPFM in 1978 and they were the ones who were actively shutting down illegal stations. As it became clear that the chairman of the FCC, William Kennard, was an advocate for licensing LPFM, the relationship between the FCC and the micro radio community became more complex. The National Association of Broadcasters (NAB) also was identified from the beginning as the Other, given the dominance of commercial radio, the rise of consolidation and the power of the broadcast lobby within the U.S. government. Two groups that emerged over time as potential Others were NPR and the Christian broadcasters. As we will see, both of these groups occupied complex, contradictory and counterintuitive spaces, forcing the MRN community to develop new discursive strategies that could integrate and respond to this complexity.

From an outside perspective, one might assume NPR would support the reestablishment of LPFM stations. Noncommercial LPFM stations could serve as outlets for NPR programming as well as a training ground for larger public radio stations' staff needs, and would expand the "public" radio presence on the radio dial. Thus, on the surface, there would appear to be a natural affinity, but this superficial connection would ignore the history of NPR and the distinctly nonlocal nature of public radio. As the micro debate gained ground within the FCC, NPR became an early and vocal opponent to any plan that would increase competition for public radio's audience and potentially interfere with radio reception. The emphatic position staked out in opposition to micro radio prompted MRN members to respond to the discursive strategies of NPR as well as the power of NPR to represent micro radio through its news media. The following analysis of the MRN discourse about NPR first addresses the activist's response to NPR's opposition and second, addresses the activists' response to NPR's framing of the micro radio issue through its news stories over this three-year period.

REACTING TO NPR: ACTIVISTS RESPOND TO NPR ATTACKS ON MICRO RADIO

Micro radio activists discussed NPR and vented their anger at NPR's opposition to LPFM throughout the three years of the MRN discussion. Beginning with an initial post about the NPR decision to oppose LPFM, the vehemence of the feelings within the micro radio community was clear. On May 13, 1998, with a subject heading, "NPR joins NAB in War on Micro Radio," Jesse Walker posted his comments and a story from *Public Broadcasting Report* about the NPR decision to oppose LPFM. "We knew about NAB, but NPR's stance, though consistent with its history and thus not a surprise, is news" (MRN post by Jesse Walker, May 13, 1998). The article Walker posted summarized NPR's April 27, 1998 comments filed with the FCC, opposing LPFM.

NPR and its affiliates support fostering a "diversity of broadcast voices." However, "it is neither self-evident nor established that diversity of media voices" will result from low-power radio. What is clear, NPR argued, is that "the broadcast spectrum in many portions of the country is severely congested," and squeezing in micro broadcasters undoubtedly would cause more interference than already occurs. (MRN post by Jesse Walker, May 13, 1998)

This article went on to address potential technical problems that would result from LPFM as current broadcasters transition to digital radio. NPR also contested the idea of the need for radio diversity by stating "that need is already being served by the Internet" (MRN post by Jesse Walker, May 13, 1998). Thus, the commercial broadcasters as represented by the NAB had a new and somewhat unlikely alliance with NPR.

The first response to the news of NPR's opposition conveys the depth of hostility this news elicited from the MRN community.

Let's rip NPR a new asshole. They are already greatly responsible for the destruction of community radio—and for the elimination of class D licenses in the first place.

As listener supported stations, they are vulnerable. Let's tell everyone who donates to withhold their donations. This is really disgusting, but typical. (MRN post by Lyn Gerry, May 13, 1998)

This visceral response puts NPR's decision in a historical context, referencing the expansion of the Corporation for Public Broadcasting (CPB) and the effects this had on community radio. This history of broadcast regulation comes out of academic scholarship, particularly McChesney (1993, 1999) and Aufderheide (1999). Gerry introduced the idea of attempting to influence NPR through a listener donation boycott campaign. This idea was followed up on by Walker. "Let's target NPR stations with roots in the community radio movement (KUSP, WYSO, etc) and community stations that carry NPR programming (an awful lot of them), asking them to publicly break with the network on the issue or else face a donor boycott" (MRN post by Jesse Walker, May 13, 1998). Though this proposal didn't generate much response at the time, the concept of an NPR boycott recurred a number of times as activists attempted to confront a potential ally turned enemy. One last contributor to this thread linked the discussion about NPR to the commercialism debate that was taking place on the MRN at about the same time. "These wannabes are social control clones. They prove to me that simply opposing commercialism will in itself usher in the New World Order" (MRN post by John vanVlaanderen, May 14, 1998). VanVlaanderen brought in the language of conspiracy as he drew attention to the fallacy of the commercial, noncommercial ideological divide. With NPR joining forces with the NAB to inhibit micro radio, the most prominent noncommercial presence on the radio dial appeared to be as protective of its audience and spectrum space as the commercial industry.

A second MRN thread that explored NPR opposition to LPFM was initiated by the release of an internal memo from NPR expressing fear of the effects of micro radio. On April 26, 1999, with the subject heading "public vs. micro," Amanda Huron, a micro radio activist from Washington, DC, posted a message she had received about NPR's anti-LPFM lobbying efforts. Huron wrote, "This just in from an anonymous friend at NPR. Managers at public radio stations are very very freaked out about low power radio" (MRN post by Amanda Huron, April 26, 1999). Huron included the text of a note that appeared to have been circulated among public radio stations. The original note came from Jennifer Ferro, assistant manager of KCRW-FM Santa Monica. The message included a response to Ferro from Alan Chartock, the executive director of WAMC/Northeast Public Radio. Alan Chartock wrote, "Jennifer: Thanks for the update. This is very, very serious stuff and we all have to do what it takes to put a stop to it" [This was in response to the following note from Jennifer Ferro] (MRN post by Amanda Huron, April 26, 1999). Ferro wrote:

I have just received a call from a board member of the NAB regarding microsations or low power FM.

He mentioned that if LPFM were to succeed, micro stations would in effect become primary and could override any translators in the area. For a station like ours, this would knock out about 30% of our service area.

Apparently a representative from KNPR in Las Vegas communicated this to members of the FCC who were surprised by this possible outcome. I was asked to write a letter explaining the effect LPFM would have on our translators and send copies to the two swing votes on the Commission, Commissioners Susan Ness and Michael Powell. (MRN post by Amanda Huron, April 26, 1999)

Thus Huron had a sample of the kind of coordination that was going on between the NAB and NPR. The concern about translators comes from the fact that many public radio stations use nonlocal transmitters to boost their signals over mountain ranges or other areas where radio reception is inhibited. If the FCC were to grant micro radio stations priority status over translators, public radio stations could lose much of their audience, as the e-mail contends. Huron then posed a question to the list:

Is it true that low-power stations could "become primary and override any translators in the area?" This isn't correct is it? (MRN post by Amanda Huron, April 26, 1999)

This question prompted a technical response.

Under the current proposal by the FCC, translators would be secondary to LP-1000 only. They would co-exist with LP-100 and LP-10. (MRN post by Michelle Eyre, April 26, 1999)

This means that the largest (1,000 watts) of the stations proposed by the FCC would have been given primary consideration over existing translators. As it turned out, the FCC amended its proposal, reducing the size of proposed low-power stations to a maximum of 100 watts, making this aspect of the debate moot.

The idea that NPR was spreading unfounded technical information was troubling to other MRN participants. One message argued that the NAB was responsible for the misinformation and public radio stations were reacting to the scare tactics.

This is obvious and blatant scare mongering by NAB. . . . I think we should go aggressively against this kind of misinformation by the NAB. . . . The NPR stations are the victims of that deception—we should exploit this to try to persuade the NPR stations not to support the NAB position. Maybe we can win some over to our side. (MRN post by Jonathan Brown, April 27, 1999)

This thread revealed that NPR's opposition to LPFM was not clearly understood. In this last post, Brown implied that NPR was not informed of the technical protections outlined by the FCC and was subject to the rumors spread by the NAB. With this, the micro radio community attempted to understand NPR's opposition, with some members arguing for a station by station appeal while others saw NPR as a historic enemy of community radio.

A more cynical perspective came from Paul Griffin:

Here is the main problem we have as I see it: None of these "authorized" stations want to give up even one watt of power. Not even the mega-watt superstations want to give up any coverage at all. Then they scream about "spectrum scarcity" and "interference issues." This is a bunch of crap. The real issue is $$$. (MRN post by Paul Griffin, April 26, 1999)

The protectionist position taken by the NAB was said to be the same defensive position taken by NPR. In fact, regardless of potential connections to community radio and the presence of the word "public" in public radio, NPR maintained and expanded their opposition to LPFM, from the drafting through the passage of the Radio Preservation Act of 2000. The critical history of broadcast regulation documented by McChesney and appropriated by some of the activists in their attempt to put the NPR decision in context, revealed itself to be a living history where the largest noncommercial voice on the FM dial closed ranks with the commercial sector (NAB) to protect their turf.

As this struggle played out on the MRN, one post responded to the discursive battle and attempted to differentiate the various contributions made by micro radio activists. This post began with a summary of a scene from the 1995 book *Green Mars*. The science fiction book by Kim Stanley Robinson was used to illustrate the point that not everyone in the movement is comfortable working through technical language ideas.

The discourse on this list is much like the colonists' plenary conference, and while I have read the competing proposals and all of your fine comments, I can't help feeling like the anarcho-colonists: while hardly an RF (radio frequency) expert, I was happier, and more effective, putting up antennae these past four years on the rooftops of the Lower East Side, running cables (and getting out of the way) than I am participating in this very technocratic thrust of the movement. (MRN post by Peter L. Spagnuolo, April 27, 1999)

Spagnuolo had a set of technical, hands-on skills he brought to the movement. His contribution as a movement intellectual was his ability to actually get a radio station on the air as opposed to engaging in nuanced discussion of the most effective strategies for promoting micro radio. With this more tangible, civil disobedience perspective, he advocated action over words.

So maybe this is the answer here—we just flood the airwaves in every city with more than their enforcement abilities can handle, and damn their proposal, with all its crumbs-from-the-table-of-capital feel. Forget fighting the govt—take it to the corporate pigs who have wrought this mess, compete head to head with them. (MRN post by Peter L. Spagnuolo, April 17, 1999)

This post was followed by support from ChuckO who wrote, "Direct action gets the goods" (MRN post by ChuckO, April 27, 1999). This support for the practical elements of the movement, the cognitive praxis, is an indication of the multiple manifestations and contributions of movement intellectuals as outlined by Eyerman and Jamison (1991). While the knowledge and discourse were pickup and refined in part through listserv discussion, practices and tangible skills were also developed and distributed throughout the community. Unlike other forms of civil disobedience where no special skills are required to carry a picket sign or march in the streets, micro radio required specific skills to build and operate a small radio station. Although it could be argued that new skills for effective lockdown have been developed by environmental protesters hoping to delay logging and mining and increasingly, street demonstrators carry gas masks and/or vinegar to mitigate the effects of pepper spray and tear gas, the protests of micro radio involved the highly technical skills of building and maintaining a small radio station. These large technical requirements necessitated a technical component to the movement, a component as powerful and necessary as the development of a media reform and democracy discourse. This thread of "public versus micro" continued with more attacks on the banality of public radio as well as support for the FCC proposal to license LPFM, acknowledging that the FCC would protect existing public radio translators.

The struggle between NPR and the micro radio activists erupted on the MRN a number of times, though the largest and most articulate thread occurred just prior to the presidential election of 2000. This time period was highly charged for all the key players in the micro radio debate, as a change of administration would mean a change of leadership at the FCC and possible redirection of the entire LPFM initiative. This extended MRN discussion of strategies for responding to NPR was initiated by a post from a couple who hoped to influence their local NPR station by threatening to withhold their annual contribution. They posted a copy of the letter they sent to their local station to the MRN.

My wife and I are great fans of public radio and recently we renewed our membership to WUFT with a $100 contribution. We did so happily but not automatically. . . . We hope to continue as regular donors to WUFT, but if NPR persists in its misguided and anti-democratic opposition to reasonable rules for licensing micropower stations, we may well reconsider our support. (MRN post by Howard Rosenfeld, October 27, 2000)

This polite letter gave the NPR debate a local face, threatening the listener support affiliates depended on. Because NPR is a national organization that relies on local affiliate stations for its membership, any campaign that created dissent among the member stations could potentially impact NPR policy. This concerned listener letter prompted a series of responses from the list that initially contributed strategic support.

Christopher Maxwell, the secretary of the Virginia Center for Public Press, Radio Free Richmond Project, responded with the names, phone numbers, and e-mail addresses of the NPR board members (MRN post by Christopher Maxwell, October 27, 2000). Another MRN user, inspired by Rosenfeld's letter, contributed her own.

Thank you Howard for writing that letter to NPR . . . and for giving me incentive to do the same. . . . Richard and I didn't contribute in our local pledge this time around and had been discussing it for awhile. Now we've made our decision. We feel badly but are sticking to our guns. (MRN post by Maryjane Stelmach Honner, October 28, 2000)

Without a formal call for a donation boycott, MRN members picked up the idea of applying pressure to local stations as one way to address NPR's opposition to LPFM. The idea of cutting off donations brought this critique from Jesse Walker:

I can't believe that I'm about to say something that might be construed as sticking up for NPR, but it might be a bit much to refuse to give money to an individual NPR station until the national network changes its tune. Perhaps it would be more effective—and more fair—to insist that the station *itself* break with national policy and endorse LPFM? (MRN post by Jesse Walker, October 28, 2000)

To which Stephen Snow added other ideas about how to apply pressure.

It seems to me there are many ways to apply pressure. One way to bring pressure to encourage an NPR affiliate to stand up for LPFM is to actively withhold support of the station . . . that is one level of pressure. There are folks doing national petitions and that's another kind of pressure. Boycotting local sponsors is another, as is boycotting NPR itself. OK, then it becomes gut-check time. If you *like* NPR generally, then you have to look inside yourself and ask which is more important. It seems to me the Internet is the perfect forum to organize a national boycott of NPR, as well as individual, localized boycotts. (MRN post by Stephen Snow, October 28, 2000)

Snow raised an issue that was woven throughout this debate. NPR was the one place on the radio dial many micro radio advocates turned to for refuge from the deluge of commercial broadcasting. The process of identifying NPR as the Other and locating effective points of opposition proved difficult for the activists. The somewhat local, somewhat progressive nature of public radio's history forced micro radio supporters to chose between standing by an established, fairly conventional public radio outlet in NPR or working for the establishment of truly local micro stations. Some saw the danger in damaging the NPR network while others had no doubt about the negative influence of homogenized public radio. Snow encapsulated these issues when he posted the following challenge to the group:

Think about the potential constituency. Are you willing to lock arms and sing "we shall overcome" with the Christian Right and others who want access to LPFM? If so, then a boycott could produce results. If you aren't, well then, there you have it. The arm twisters who manipulate government *count* on dissent being fragmented. Organized dissent they cannot handle. (MRN post by Stephen Snow, October 28, 2000)

True to form, Jesse Walker responded,

Actually, I hate NPR. I'm all for locking arms with right-wing religious nuts. I'm merely observing that we're never going to convince the national network to switch sides on this one, but we might persuade a group of independent minded stations to break with NPR loudly and publicly. It's a matter of more bang for your withheld buck. (MRN post by Jesse Walker, October 29, 2000)

Two other posts responded to this thread with comments about the consolidation that had occurred within public radio. Alan Freed, a micro broadcaster from Beat Radio in Minneapolis, noted how Minnesota Public Radio owns "29 stations and 18 translators in seven states" (MRN post by Alan Freed, October 28, 2000). K. Coan added,

The same NPR network programming is duplicated on (three stations in the Cleveland area) . . . it is a waste of the spectrum and that's what I hear every morning. Oh it's great if you want to compare the processing of each signal, but that's where the public service ends. (MRN post by K Coan, October 29, 2000)

The activists confronted the limitations of the current public broadcasting arrangement at the same time that they looked at who their allies were in the debate. The movement's need to identify an Other was contingent upon the identification of "us." Not only was NPR a problematic opponent because of their (limited) connection to local noncommercial radio, but the supporters of LPFM encompassed a wide range of ideological agendas that made alliances less than obvious.

The previous thread, under the subject heading "our contribution" was redirected by a post from Ted Coopman with the subject heading, "worth the time?" Coopman wrote:

I guess it would come down to what would be the point of the exercise, what is our goal? Is it to punish/destroy NPR? Is it to out NPR as a propaganda tool run by professional propagandists? Is it to incite reform at NPR (is reform even possible?) Incite revolution in the ranks (would NPR affiliates do anything to degrade the image of their biggest cash cow?)? All of them? None?

I have my own favorites on this list. . . . Would our resources be spent better elsewhere?

Would this be another distraction or is it an important lynch pin in the larger media democracy revolution? (MRN post by Ted Coopman, October 29, 2000)

Coopman raised the question of efficacy as well as the larger context of the media and democracy project. These questions elicited a number of responses from the micro radio community. Most of the posts addressed specific strategies for confronting NPR on the issue.

Sarah Ferguson responded with a series of specific tactics to apply to NPR as the micro radio community began to realize the need to confront an "ally" turned "Other."

While I think unpledging is a strong tactic, it seems we need to do something now to raise attention to the NPR sellouts—who get tons of corporate underwriting anyway.

What about a fax blast to NPR and relevant media outlets demanding that they change their tune. . . .

I think a well-worded screed, with demands, could embarrass them further. . . .

Can anyone, Petri, Mike Bracy, Stephan, etc, undertake such a task of drafting a letter with our demand(s) which would go to Kevin Klose and associates at the national level? (MRN post by Sarah Fergurson, October 30, 2000)

Ferguson advocated a two-pronged strategy of directly confronting the NPR board while raising public awareness about NPR's position on the issue. Her request for a drafted letter was answered the next day.

Pete triDish from the Prometheus Radio Project posted a draft of a detailed letter to the NPR board. This letter addressed the ideological and the technical reasons for endorsing LPFM as well as the potential support LPFM could offer to NPR. This letter was cosigned by Andrea Buffa of the Media Alliance, Peter Franck of the National Lawyers Guild Committee on Democratic Communication, and Glenn Austin of Americans for Radio Diversity.

Dear NPR board members,

With heavy hearts, we regret to inform you that there will be a demonstration and press conference outside your board meeting this Saturday to tell the public about NPR's campaign to defeat low power radio. Throughout the movement to create a low power radio service, there has been great reluctance to confront NPR on this issue: many of us are loyal NPR listeners and subscribers.

The demands for more studies on this issue are a transparent attempt to delay until a change of administration would derail the low power plan all together. NPR should be ashamed to be an accomplice to this anti-competitive endeavor, and the time has come that NPRs' listeners and contributors must know.

We will be asking that listeners withhold their donations to NPR affiliates that oppose low power radio. . . . The arrogance of power and incumbency must be challenged wherever it manifests.

We will be happy to discuss our position and our actions with members of the NPR board. We hope that NPR can reconnect with its mission of public service and cast aside its competitive, corporate, and condescending attitude towards the public that it is entrusted with serving. We hope that we will be able to call off our campaign as soon as NPR chooses to exhibit good faith towards the emerging community radio movement. We are sorry that it had to come to this. (MRN post by Pete triDish, October 30, 2000)

TriDish and the others who signed this letter detailed their position on the issue and made their case for why LPFM and NPR were complementary, not mutually exclusive. The tone of this letter was an indication of the mixed feelings within the micro radio community and reflected the complicated process of defining NPR as the oppositional Other.

Walker responded in support of Petri's letter, though he noted that the efficacy of "unpledging" resided with those who *do* pledge. "It's beside the point if, like me, you don't give money to NPR, reserving your radio pledge dollars for independent community stations and student-run college stations" (MRN post by Jesse Walker, October 30, 2000). David Huff, a micro broadcaster from Canyon Lake Radio also offered support for confronting NPR, especially using the idea of a "fax-blast." Though he liked the idea of action, he also posted words of caution and suspicion.

As it is safe to assume, (indeed foolhardy to ignore the likelihood!) that this list is being closely monitored by certain hostile agencies and organizations, I would suggest that a few of us arrange for a conference call to discuss this matter further, and soon.

Anyone interested in participating in such a conference, please contact me at the following address. (MRN post by David Huff, October 31, 2000)

This post acknowledged the power of the Internet to coordinate people across great distances. The same open structure that allowed new micro radio enthusiasts to join the MRN also allowed for monitoring and surveillance by corporate and government agencies. As coordination around this campaign became more specific, off-line communication was used to limit the potential for surveillance. The Internet proved to be a powerful coordinating tool although the activists were aware of the privacy concerns embodied in on-line communication.

Jay Hamilton, a professor from the Grady College of Journalism and Mass Communication at the University of Georgia, voiced his support for pressuring individual stations:

All good tactics—yet Sarah's suggestion to begin to try to split local affiliates from network policy or at least to encourage them to put pressure on the stance of NPR would hit the network directly (what's a network w/o local affiliates?). (MRN post by Jay Hamilton, October 31, 2000)

As a university professor, Hamilton represented a voice familiar with academic discourse. A number of other people posted short notes supporting these suggestions for confronting NPR. In spite of the chorus of support, Ted Coopman was not satisfied that the micro radio community had thought through the issue. Coopman offered the following analogy:

Most NPR affiliates are like drug addicts when it comes to NPR programming. NPR programming draws a lot of funding from businesses and the public, but costs more and more money each year (up 30% this last year alone). So stations need to build translators to increase their audience and focus on programming that draws people to listen. This is usually NPR programming, which costs more money, which requires more translators, which cost more money, which requires more NPR programming, and so on. (MRN post by Ted Coopman, October 31, 2000)

And to illustrate an unspoken issue running through this entire debate about NPR, Coopman added the following political analogy:

To put forth a timely analogy, NPR is like the Democratic Party. Compared to commercial media (Republicans) it seems liberal and for most people it is the only game in town. LPFM advocates are like the Greens, and will be seen as "splitting progressive media" by going after NPR. As the Dem's/liberals might say, "by attacking NPR we weaken it and could cause a loss of funding in Congress and endanger noncommercial radio. It might even lead to a take over by right wing religious broadcasters! We should work with NPR because the opposition/alternative is so much worse."

Again, do we want to get bogged down in a slugfest with NPR? Do they deserve it?

I think they do.

But what do we hope to gain? Revenge? A complete reversal on the LPFM issue? Do we think this is possible?

By doing this are we really moving forward Media Democracy or are we just jacking-off? (MRN post by Ted Coopman, October 31, 2000)

Coopman continued to push the issue of efficacy. The comparison of micro radio to the Green party was an articulation of the "conflict" many micro radio advocates had previously expressed about confronting NPR.

Chris Maxwell from Radio Free Richmond responded to Coopman point by point, largely agreeing with his analysis. He saw division within the NPR board over the micro radio issue.

I have heard that this was the most contentious issue to face an NPR board in decades, so they are apparently NOT unified . . . and there are affiliates such as WHRV/WHRO in Norfolk that really work on being responsive to the community yet still have NPR national programming. (MRN post by Christopher Maxwell, October 31, 2000)

Regarding Coopman's assertion that they should work with NPR because the opposition/alternative was much worse, Maxwell responded, "There are still quite a number of community radio stations out there and even some commercial radio stations that actually do an amazing job!" (MRN post by Christopher Maxwell, October 31, 2000). Maxwell attempted to limit the rhetoric of generalization. His post demonstrated an ability to see the Other not as an institution (NPR) but as support for policies that limit public access to the media. Responding to Coopman's final question about advancing the cause or jacking-off, Maxwell wrote:

Aye, that IS the million dollar question. I suppose that for as long as this budget rider battle drags on and on and on . . . that if we could get some affiliates and underwriters to contact

President Clinton, McCain etc. and show them NPR's position is NOT monolithic and based on misleading "evidence" . . . then maybe we can cauterize the wound caused by Kevin "Judas" Klose a bit . . . maybe just enough. (MRN post by Christopher Maxwell, October 31, 2000)

Again, Maxwell is arguing for a complex vision of the institutions engaged in the struggle. NPR is "NOT monolithic." Drawing attention to the discontinuities, Maxwell attempted to prevent the movement from seeing all large institutions as potential, totalizing, homogeneous threats. Instead, he attempted to point out the gaps and cracks, places where organizations live and breathe.

Pete triDish followed this line of thinking, supporting an agenda of gradual change. Pete wrote:

Just because the first time you confront someone powerful they don't do what you asked them to do, does not mean that your campaign is not effective.

NPR is vulnerable, and sometimes when you step on a giants toes, they switch to your side or at least move out of the way. If anyone should know that, we do. Right now, we have an FCC chairman who is jumping up and down and screaming about a "plot by the broadcasters" (his words). Who thought that would happen three years ago? What's exciting about this is that we don't have guaranteed outcomes—I can't promise you that we can force NPR out of the way, but I'm willing to bet a little bit of my effort that we can. (MRN post by Pete triDish, October 31, 2000)

TriDish brought the history of the micro movement to bear on this subject, reminding the group that major changes had already taken place in part because of the work of the activist community and that NPR was just another large obstacle in the path. Apparently this type of discussion was what Coopman had hoped to initiate because he followed this series of messages by writing, "Thanks Pete and everyone, that was what I was looking for" (MRN post by Ted Coopman, October 31, 2000).

Although not every addition to this thread was summarized here, the selected messages provide a glimpse of the community of activists nationwide working through the complex process of identifying and responding to a formidable Other. NPR posed complex questions for the micro radio community and this exchange reveals a group of movement intellectuals, each bringing a different set of skills and knowledge to the table, working through the nuances of a difficult problem.

RESPONDING TO REPRESENTATION: ACTIVISTS CRITIQUE NPR'S COVERAGE OF MICRO RADIO

For any social movement, the issue of representation is critical to the dissemination of movement knowledge. The media activism and reform movement in general and the micro radio issue in particular are unique in that one of the central issues of the movement is the ability of the movement to represent itself to a wide audience through modern communication technology. Micro radio was a struggle about access to low-power radio technology. With access comes the ability to determine one's own representation; control over the objectification process. The struggle between NPR and micro radio was unique in this regard in that the activists were well aware of the power of radio to shape stories. The micro radio activists, like most social movements, were denied direct access to the dominant communication media. Residue of this tension can be found in the activist's critique of the way NPR covered the micro radio issue.

Eyerman and Jamison (1991) have commented on the tension between mass media and social movements, noting the impact of television on the emergence of movement professionals. Previous movements were said to rely on media professionals because of the high cost of creating and distributing media products that supported the movement's agenda. In the case of micro radio, the movement *included* rather than *employed* media professionals, and these professionals played a significant role in determining the media coverage, as we will see in the next chapter. What follows is not the mediated voices of industry professionals, but rather the reaction of activists as they critique their portrayal by NPR, an organization that remained a problematic opponent.

On August 25, 1998, NPR aired a report on "Morning Edition" about an FCC crackdown on micro broadcasters in Miami that resulted in the closure of fifteen stations in the area. J. F. Noonan heard the report and posted this comment question to the MRN:

FCC flack claimed interference with air traffic control radio was one of the concerns about the unlicensed broadcasts. (Does anybody know what frequencies the FAA uses? Is it even vaguely possible that a 5 watt station broadcasting between 88-108 MHz could interfere?). (MRN post by J. F. Noonan, August 25, 1998)

Xavier from the International Workers of the World responded with technical information as well as comments about the framing of the story.

An FM station that is putting out "spurs" or breaking into oscillations at those frequencies could cause problems.

It should be pointed out that the FCC/NAB plays the "air traffic interference" card to inflame public sentiments. . . . The FCC/NAB is trying to invoke visions of the fiery deaths of hundreds of women and children in the minds of the docile public. It's our job to help the public to not be so docile.

The amateur radio folks are self policing we should be able to do the same. (MRN post by Xavier, August 26, 1998)

MikeB weighed in with his expertise:

The civilian radio frequencies for ATC (air traffic control) are in the 118 MHz to 121 MHz on the VHF side. . . . I'd say the argument was pretty much baloney unless someone was deliberately broadcasting up into that range. (MRN post by MikeB, August 26, 1998)

Coopman noted how this issue has come up before and there was little substantiation to the charge of micro radio interfering with air traffic control.

Unintentional interference of air traffic control transmissions has never been proven in court against a micro radio station to my knowledge or to my knowledge have there been official complaints from pilots.

The FCC/NAB like to frame it as a safety issue, and it is. Keeping the monopoly safe from 99% of the population. (MRN post by Ted Coopman, August 27, 1998)

Jesse Walker followed this comment by posting a transcript of the NPR piece, allowing the entire list to read the story and draw their own conclusions.

REPRESENTING PROTEST: NPR COVERS A DEMONSTRATION

On October 5, 1998, micro radio activists held a demonstration in Washington, DC, in front of the offices of the FCC, followed by a parade to the offices of the NAB. This colorful protest included large puppets depicting FCC Chairman William Kennard as a Pinocchio puppet manipulated by the strings of an "NAB" puppet, who was in turn manipulated by the strings of a green pyramid representing corporate America. The entire protest was illegally broadcast from a micro radio transmitter hidden in one of the protestor's backpacks. The protest was the culmination of a weekend micro radio conference that included the launch of a micro station in the Mt. Pleasant neighborhood of DC. NPR covered the protest on "All Things Considered" and their news story prompted this response from Ed Armstrong of Radio Limbo in Tucson, Arizona:

I had the good fortune today to get to hear the NPR report on the DC microradio event on All Things Considered. They played the setup of the transmitter that took place last night and they interviewed Pete Tridish and a couple of other folks.

It was charming, hearing the new micro station come up for the first time. All in all, it presented the micro radio movement in a reasonably positive light. (MRN post by Edwin Armstrong, Jr., October 5, 1998)

A few others posted queries and the Internet links to the "RealAudio" files on the NPR web site. Jesse Walker posted a transcript of the news piece. Finally, Bill Smolenske from Free Radio Santa Barbara added his critique:

I thought the NPR piece was pretty weak. It was good to get some coverage about our movement but it really lacked details about the movement that the general public need to know. I give it a C-. Many thanks to all who participated in DC. You guys and gals are the new revolutionaries as our forefathers were, fighting for freedom. (MRN post by Bill Smolenske, October 7, 1998)

The community appeared pleased to have received coverage for their demonstration and because of NPR's national coverage, micro broadcasters across the country were able to hear about the DC protest. Although there was not a lot of commentary about the coverage, transcripts and links to the Internet audio file were posted that allowed people who missed the story to listen to or read the coverage. This NPR coverage and the activists response reveals the complexity and the tensions in the relationship between the movement and the media.

NPR AND IN-DEPTH COVERAGE: "TALK OF THE NATION" TAKES ON MICRO RADIO

The NPR piece that received the most feedback from the micro radio activists was a "Talk of the Nation" episode that featured Andrew Schwartzman from the Media Access Project and Stephen Dunifer from Free Radio Berkeley. William Kennard was supposed to be a guest on the program but he declined when he heard Dunifer was to be included, citing the ongoing lawsuit between the FCC and Dunifer. Prior to the show, Diane Fleming, a micro broadcaster who called herself the "Condom Lady" because of her micro radio program that promoted safe sex education, posted an alert about the upcoming show:

Hi All, get your comments ready for Talk of the Nation at 2:00 pm today. Looks like the panel will be all men, so I am especially encouraging the women of radio to call . . . 1-800-989-8255 . . . keep trying if it's busy! (MRN post by Diane Fleming, December 7, 1998)

After the show, Kvaack posted a note about how to continue to weigh in on this issue:

Awesome show IMO, [Internet slang: In My Opinion] Don't forget that there is a message board on the NPR web site that we need to represent our self on. Also, thank you notes are a nice touch: totn@npr.org. (MRN post by Kvaak, December 7, 1998)

Jerry, a micro broadcaster from GRID radio in Cleveland, Ohio had a more critical perspective on the "Talk of the Nation" program.

We ARE making a difference. Just the fact that we were in NPR. It did seem obvious that that the host was a bit lopsided in favor of NPR's position on micro radio.

I know the world as a whole is crumbling fast. Faster than most people realize, but let's not give in to those who would oppress us. With each passing day our rights are more and more restricted. Micro radio will pave the way to educating the public about the truth. The truth that the NABs and the NPRs will not air. For as we know, the truth will set us free! (MRN post by JSGRID, December 7, 1998)

This post contained another expression of affirmation for the appearance of micro radio on a national program despite the fact that the program was produced by an oppositional organization. NPR was grouped with the NAB as a censor of "the truth." Given the divergent perspectives between the micro broadcasters and NPR, "the truth" of broadcast policy could be seen as dependent on having a place on the dial!

Chuck Munson (aka: ChuckO) echoed the previous comments from Jerry, adding critique of the type of information emphasized on the show. Munson's critique was that the policy issues superceded the "practices" of the micro broadcasters, moving the debate into the realm of regulatory politics and away from the grassroots communities where the micro stations actions were felt.

I was a bit disappointed with the broadcast, but happy that it happened. Dunifer came across as an articulate, knowledgeable guy. The FCC looked bad by not even bothering to show up for a debate.

I was disappointed that the NPR guy managed to keep part of the show focused on the FCC's authority to regulate the airwaves.

It was nice to hear Diane got through. I wish the show could have focused more on what people are doing with their communities. Fortunately, we did hear a little bit about what FRB [Free Radio Berkley] did on the air. It's just like fucking NPR to keep most of the discussion on Beltway-style politics. (MRN post by Chuck Munson, December 7, 1998)

Jerry from GRID radio added a note of support for Chuck's post, and a number of other posts traded information for listening to the show on the Internet.

These MRN threads about the NPR coverage of the micro radio issue reflect the complex relationship between the micro broadcasters and NPR. On one hand they are pleased to have the national exposure and at the same time there is frustration at the way the topic was framed. NPR offered extended radio news pieces that reached a potentially sympathetic audience for the micro radio movement. At the same time, NPR's leadership actively opposed the FCC's plan to license micro radio. This combination of potentially sympathetic audience with an adversarial management required the activists to debate and work through how to confront this ally turned opponent. These threads reveal the MRN community struggling to define effective strategies for responding to NPR, and shows them only occasionally agreeing on methods and tactics.

CHRISTIAN COMMUNITY: MICRO FRIENDS OR MEGALITH ENEMIES

Christian broadcasters posed a complex series of questions for the micro radio community. In their quest for space on the FM dial, micro broadcasters challenged the dominant radio industry. Part of that industry was made up of Christian commercial and noncommercial stations. Many of these stations were owned and operated by a few large organizations, including the American Family Association (AFA) and the Calvary Chapel of Twin Falls. These large broadcasting companies, sometimes referred to as "satellite-ers," distribute syndicated programming through their network of radio and television stations. The national presence of these Christian groups on the radio dial, combined with largely nonlocal programming, put this segment of the Christian community in the same category as the NAB.

In contrast to this, a number of small churches across the country had participated in micro radio civil disobedience by going on the air in violation of FCC policy. These small churches and religious groups operated micro stations such as Prayze FM in Hartford, Connecticut, and used the same set of legal defenses established in the Dunifer case to defend their actions. These religious groups shared the goals of the micro broadcasters and used the same tactics of direct action broadcasting to demonstrate their message.

The Christian community embodied another set of contradictions for the micro broadcasters. A large, well-organized and well-funded arm of the Christian community posed a threat to micro radio in their ability to file applications and fund new low power stations that could then repeat programming that was centrally produced and distributed. In contrast, the smaller churches that had picked up the low-power banner presented a strategic alliance for the micro broadcasters. As the struggle over LPFM moved into the halls of Congress, representatives (particularly Republicans) were faced with a difficult choice given their sympathy to the concerns of the NAB and their support base among the Christian community, large churches and small. With small churches joining the call for LPFM, the image of the micro broadcasters moved beyond a group of anarchists and leftists to include members of the religious right.

One of the issues that united the opposition to LPFM from both the Christian broadcasters and NPR was the issue of radio station translators. The Christian broadcasters used a great deal of syndicated programming distributed via satellite and repeated across translators. In the initial LPFM proposal, it was unclear whether the FCC would give preference to those stations already operating a translator, or if the translator frequency could be displaced by a micro station offering local programming. In the final "Report and Order," the FCC chose to protect existing translators, though future expansions would be subject to competition from LPFM applicants. In the case of NPR and the established Christian broadcasters, both groups desired as much protection of existing and future translators as a way to guarantee audience expansion. The micro broadcasters on the other hand, while acknowledging the value of translators, tended to argue that local programming was more likely to serve the local public interest.

As the micro radio community worked to define the Other, they were forced to distinguish between the Christians represented by the likes of the American Family Association and the Christians associated with smaller churches who wanted to speak to their congregations and communities for the same reasons the micro broadcasters wanted access to the airwaves. Making the distinction between these two groups proved difficult for the micro radio community. The MRN listserv provided a snapshot of the range of opinions and ideas about the relationship between the activists and the faithful (and the faithful activists!) and revealed the intimate process of identifying movement allies and opponents.

CHRISTIAN ALLIES: THE UNITED CHURCH OF
CHRIST AND THE MEDIA ACCESS PROJECT

One example of the complex relationship between the micro radio activists and the Christian community was the coordination of efforts between the Media Access Project (MAP) and The United Church of Christ (UCC). These two organizations worked together to create statements that were submitted to the FCC that reflected the concerns of both the activists and part of the Christian community. This cooperation, between an institutional piece of the media activism and reform movement and a mainstream (although not evangelical) Christian organization, contrasts with the suspicious and heated dialogue among the activists on the MRN listserv. In their combined comments to the FCC, MAP and the UCC wrote:

To ensure that low power radio does not become a replica of currently-existing services, UCC, et al. call upon the Commission to require that half of each low power radio station's programming be locally originated. UCC, et al. also insist that the Commission adopt ownership limits that will ensure that the low power radio service can add diverse and independent perspectives to the marketplace of ideas. (http://www.mediaaccess.org/programs/lpfm/cosumm.html)

Throughout their comments, the UCC and MAP supported the same discourse the activists had been promoting. This cooperative and mutually agreed upon set of ideas was in contrast to the discourse around the involvement of the Christian community on the MRN, and the fears expressed about the potential takeover of LPFM by big commercial broadcasters. The following examples of discussion on the MRN reveal the intensity of the feelings wrapped up in the issue of religious broadcasting and allows for a glimpse into the process of the MRN subscribers working through totalizing conceptions to reach more nuanced understandings of an emerging constituency of the media activism and reform movement.

CHRISTIANS: MICRO RADIO FRIENDS *AND* FOES

Discussion about the Christian community appeared sporadically throughout the three years of MRN discussion examined in this study. This section will examine one short thread and then one longer thread where MRN participants engaged in discussion about the influence of the Christian community on LPFM. The first short thread took place in March 1999 and demonstrated attempts by the activists to enlist the help of *some* Christian organizations in their fight for LPFM.

Tom Ness, the owner and publisher of a local music magazine in Michigan, *Jamrag,* posted a note to the MRN about his efforts to recruit the help of local churches.

Tonight we mailed out kits to 100 local churches and church groups. We enclosed a support letter written by a well-known local bishop, Thomas Gumbleton. Gumbleton was recently in the news for his many trips to Iraq bringing medicine in violation of the sanctions. We're asking the churches to file comments in favor of the FCC's plan. (MRN post by Tom Ness, March 12, 1999)

This post was followed by a series of questions about the Bishop's affiliations and denomination from Don Schellhardt, the National Coordinator of the Amherst Alliance. Tom Ness responded to these questions with comments that indicate the tenuous nature of any alliance between the activists and the Christian community.

You're talking to a hardcore atheist here. . . . All I know for certain is he is always first in line to stand up for the little guy, especially those hated by society; i.e. AIDS patients, Iraqi children, etc.

I hope our mailing is not construed as taking the AFA [American Family Association] thing lightly. Some of those AFA folks would burn an atheistic, pot-smoking fag like me at the stake! We're trying to lobby the churches because their support adds a certain legitimacy to our movement. And we're looking for an angle to win over these Republicans who largely control our destiny (like it or not). But I'm also scared to death of anyone—especially fundamentalist Christians—from building monopolistic media empires. (MRN post by Tom Ness, March 12, 1999)

Ness's comments are an example of the activists working through the process of building political support while defending the technology that inspired the movement. His fears about personal persecution as well as anxieties about larger "monopolistic" domination are two themes repeated throughout the discourse around the involvement of the Christian community.

Responding to Ness's fears of Christian media empires, Christopher Maxwell argued for LPFM rules that require stations to be operated by local organizations that do not already own media outlets.

They might be fundamentalists but they will have to operate as we would. They would also be nationally limited to one station per organization. That would at least slow down the Chain McChurches. Also, even within the fundamentalist movement, there is a diversity of viewpoints. I find that a lot of fundamentalists believe in the same thing as "progressives" once you get them away from the big national orgs that are essentially front groups for corporations. Like a suit in a Jesus outfit. (MRN post by Christopher Maxwell, March 12, 1999)

Maxwell hoped that the FCC rules would limit the ability of powerful Christian media organizations to dominate the new LPFM service. Thus as an activist, he was putting a measure of faith (!) in the regulatory agency that the activist community as a whole had worked so hard to change. In this instance, the FCC moved from an oppositional force to a potential ally with the power to mitigate the influence of power and money.

This thread concluded with a post from Amanda Huron, an activist working with Mt. Pleasant Radio in Washington, DC. Huron's post shows the activists using the MRN as a coordinating tool, sharing ideas and resources for moving the LPFM issue forward on a national basis.

Could you post the text of a sample support letter from a church? The group I'm with that's starting a station is closely aligned with a local (radical) church and we are going to be getting support letters from many different community organizations, including churches. It would be helpful to see the kind of wording you are using. I think churches can be incredible organizing bodies, and we need to work to get them and their energy and resources on our side. (MRN post by Amanda Huron, March 14, 1999)

Ness responded to Huron's request by posting the text of the letter of support he had drafted and Bishop Gumbleton from the Archdiocese of Detroit had signed. It is interesting to note Huron's designation of the church she was working with as "radical," a sign that she was aware of the concerns about the AFA and other large, mainstream Christian organizations. At the same time, Huron affirmed the potential organizing power of churches and added her support for enlisting their help in the LPFM cause.

A second major debate about the influence of the Christian community erupted after a front page *New York Times* article covered the tension between the Christian supporters of LPFM and the reading service for the blind. The International Association of Audio Services (IAAS) oversees radio services to the blind. These services are carried on frequencies located very close to the station frequencies they serve (these are often referred to as subcarrier frequencies and special radios are needed to receive IAAS services). The concern of the IAAS was that low-power radio would cause interference or potentially eliminate the reading service altogether. This put IAAS in opposition to the micro radio service and thus at odds with many small churches hoping to access LPFM. The *New York Times* article noted that in the first round of applications for low-power licenses, half the applicants were churches. The news article raised the question of the potential conflict between Christians and the blind. This issue prompted the following response:

A large spectrum handout to conservative/fundamentalist religious communities is not what we've been putting our asses on the line for and doesn't meet the requirements of the Free Radio Austin Mission Statement.

Until LPFMers *themselves* can hammer out a collective consensus on a good plan, we will be stuck with whatever shit they decide we should have. (MRN post by the slave, July 13, 2000)

This elicited a response from Jesse Walker:

Lots of Christian broadcasters put their asses on the line by transmitting illegally, just like you have. I'd doubt they'd want to be part of your consensus. (MRN post by Jesse Walker, July 13, 2000)

To which The Slave responded:

And those Christians deserve to be hung on every cross we can nail them to. They are trying to monopolize and take advantage of an LPFM movement that was supposed to be about *opening* access so that the community can use it but these jerks want to *close* access and limit it to the same narrow-minded religious dogma and anti-intellectualism that has mired and collared this nation for centuries.

If the LPFM movement as a whole embraces the same philosophy you do with regard to the religious right-wing, then I would have to say fuck that LPFM movement.

Stations around the nation aren't risking fines, lawyers fees, and trial after trial just so they can turn around and hand over the new LPFM spectrum to the same old fire-and-brimstone fundamentalist nutsoids that made the U.S. a really lame place to live in the 1950s. They can eat my shit. Fuck em. (MRN post by The Slave, July 13, 2000)

This post was then parodied by DJ Dizzy. DJ Dizzy repeated The Slave's post almost word for word, only replacing "Christian" with "Punk Rockers." DJ Dizzy used sarcasm to try to point out the danger of vilifying one group in the defense of "community." The Slave responded to this parody with:

I wish I wuz so cool and open minded like youse dj Dizzy. If I was, then after handing half the bandwidth to Christians, then I could be liberal, hip and open minded enough to hand over the *other* half to da neo-nazies. (MRN post by The Slave, July 13, 2000)

DJ Dizzy attempted to explain his message.

The point was, you could plug any group—punk rockers, dope fiends, pineapple eaters, Asians, people who live in Austin, any group—into your rant and it would make just as much sense.

I didn't personally attack you, just satirized your post so that maybe you would understand that those religious fanatics—who have nothing in common with this atheist—have just as much right to the airwaves as anyone else. (MRN post by DJ Dizzy, July 13, 2000)

Thus we see a familiar pattern repeat itself. This idea showed up in the debate over commercialism and was an ongoing part of the process of working through the substantive issues of the movement. This pattern consists of the discussion of an idea or concept that at first appears to be homogeneous and totalizing but after debate, turns out to be complex and not easily identified as friend or enemy.

Jesse Walker again responded to The Slave and made the case for seeing the value of the Christian community's contribution to the LPFM movement. In response to The Slave's comment, "They can eat my shit," Walker wrote:

Can I have some of that yummy fecal matter, too? 'Cause I'm happy to be allied with Christians who risked fines, lawyers fees, and trial after trial to legalize micro radio, same as the leftists did. I also understand that there's a difference between handing over all the LPFM spectrum to churches (which isn't happening) and letting churches be among the LPFM applicants (which is)

I also know that it's good politics to have churches on your side. I guarantee you that phones are ringing in GOP Senators' offices because of the *Times* article and that the angry callers are conservative constituents who ordinarily vote Republican. (MRN post by Jesse Walker, July 13, 2000)

The Slave then became the most vocal anti-Christian voice on the MRN, articulating not only his opposition to religious domination of the airwaves but also a rabid, one might say fundamentalist, opposition to religion in general. He responded to each of his critics and his critics multiplied as his posts became more vitriolic. Richard Edmondson of San Francisco Liberation Radio tried to point out the historic connection of some Christians to social welfare movements when he wrote,

Christianity is not all monolithic and evil as you think. One of my friends is a nun. She has organized numerous protests on behalf of homeless people, she has committed civil disobedience and gone to jail on numerous occasions. If people like her want to run their own radio stations, I have no problem with it. (MRN post by Richard Edmondson, July 14, 2000)

And DJ Dizzy added this:

I agree that there are concerns. We all know about the corporate religious stations hi-jacking others' applications. But mom and pop churches are one of the main groups to get the whole thing going. And having FCC cops busting into churches has been great publicity for our cause. Having churches on our side has made the mainstreamers who might look down their noses on the punk rockers realize this is an important issue. (MRN post by DJ Dizzy, July 14, 2000)

The Slave responded to all these posts individually. Answering Edmondson's post about the diversity within the Christian community, The Slave wrote,

I disagree with you. Christians suck. Sure, there are a few nice ones that do some really nice progressive things . . . but nothing takes away from the fact that they are Christians and have a faith in a book of illogical lies. That lack of logic is sure to spill over into their personal lives. . . . Religion remains the stonghold of morons. Religion is your enemy whether you chose to believe it or not. (MRN post by The Slave, July 14, 2000)

In response to Jesse Walker's comments about coalition building and the value of supporting Christian inclusion in the LPFM movement, The Slave launched into an extended diatribe about the discourse process taking place on the MRN.

What I see is an avoidance of issues on this list. There is a consistent lack of real discussion on this. Your arguments, while expressed clearly and succinctly, don't impress me one bit. Basically, it's "hey man, whatever dude!" type of argument that avoids the issue altogether. It's like first come, first serve, but this isn't Shoney's Jesse, there is a limited supply of bandwidth available . . . and how to divvy up that limited resource is gonna fall on someone's shoulders.

What most on the MRN list would rather do, it seems, is rather than dealing with REAL politics and discussion, is just leave it up to the FCC to figure out what LPFM "means," then divvy up the license accordingly.

And there's quite a bit of politicking here rather than alienate some potential allies, like fundamentalist loonies, you would rather have them on your side to fight the valiant LPFM cause. Personally, with friends like that, who needs enemies.

Sincerely, if it came down to an LPFM with 50% Christians, and no LPFM at all, I'd rather take no LPFM at all and fuck the whole deal. It's not worth my time and energy (in fact it's a big waste) working on LPFM if half of it goes to the looney-fringe nutsoids that call themselves Christians. (MRN post by The Slave, July 14, 2000)

Responding to Walker's assertion that an alliance with the Christians was politically expedient because of the links between the Republican party and the Christian community, The Slave wrote,

I really don't give a damn about the GOP or what they think. It's not about that shit anyway . . . it's about the NAB. It was years ago and it is today. It's about money, not beliefs. The only thing you *might* get out of this type of politicking is a new LPFM bill aimed *soley* at opening LPFM Christian stations. Now that would be rich. Outside of that, it's the ceaseless struggle against the cogs of the capitalist machine that rolls over all life, squeezes blood from the planet, and makes every living thing an automaton and an object to be bought and sold. (MRN post by The Slave, July 14, 2000)

This post from The Slave was indicative of a segment of the micro broadcasting community that was not interested in step by step political reform. These people tended to advocate an unregulated "free radio" model where citizens could broadcast at will and the government would serve only to moderate disputes. Despite the overt support for LPFM from FCC Chairman Kennard, The Slave and many others remained suspicious of any government regulation. Putting this in a strictly political and economic context, The Slave rejected the arguments for cultural diversity, instead embracing a model of struggle between the haves and have nots.

Walker responded to this post by questioning how Christian stations might be limited and who would be responsible for making these allocations. While The Slave appeared to advocate some form of percentage system according to the type of organization applying for the license, Walker, in classic libertarian form, advocated for local control of these decisions.

What's appropriate in one city might not be appropriate in others. In some towns, there'll be room for both religious and non-religious LPFMs. In other towns, only religious (or non-religious) groups will apply. It yet other towns, there'll be conflicts, and that's the only time your questions enter the picture . . . except that even there it isn't necessarily a zero sum game, or at least not as much of one, since the different groups could (and should) share the frequency. (MRN post by Jesse Walker, July 15, 2000)

Walker embraced a model based around local control, though he also appeared optimistic that communities would "share" station time among the diverse community constituents. The arguments contained in this on-line debate, though largely driven by a small group of participants, nevertheless contained many issues that were central to the evolution of this movement and were also indicative of movement growth and development as a whole. These discussions also provide an intimate, detailed glimpse of the specific, historically contingent exchanges that take place within a movement. The MRN was one place where the broad range of "movement intellectuals" interacted and worked together to explore the details of the emerging cognitive terrain. The developmental process of the micro radio discourse can be seen in The Slave's response to Walker:

As a free radio movement comes closer to actual implementation, one has to look at the concrete details and begin to ask how the one would implement an LPFM scheme. The idea that just any factionalized group should be allowed a station on a willy-nilly, first come, first serve basis, in a world of limited bandwidth seems immature. If LPFMers are serious about getting what they want, then they need to get together and hammer out what they want from the government in concrete terms. If you *don't* hammer out the details, then they will by default be left to the FCC and the NAB to define. Over time, you will find yourselves once again disenfranchised and back where you started. (MRN post by The Slave, July 16, 2000)

This post went on with another round of Christian denunciations from The Slave, as well as point by point responses to Walker's arguments. The extreme tone of the thread elicited a response from Philip Tymon, a lawyer at the National Lawyers Guild, who tried to encourage MRN members to stick to micro radio related topics and move philosophical debates "off-list."

It amazes me that people on this list seem to completely lose perspective in the real world and think that just because they sent a few e-missives they are having some impact on the world. Sorry to tell you, there are a quarter billion people in this country. A large number of them identify themselves as right-wing Christians. . . . There is a strategic issue here and it can be solved with serious thought, wisdom and patience. Temper tantrums and simplistic religious debates are just a waste of time. I don't want to be your captive audience. Please go away. (MRN post by Philip Tymon, July 16, 2000)

The irony in this post is that it is only Tymon's definition of "serious thought" that will move the issue forward as opposed to the open discussion that had been taking place. Tymon's position is even more contradictory given his work with the National Lawyers Guild Committee on Democratic Communication. Tymon's post is another example of the difficulty of defining and then practicing "democratic communication." Thus, we see yet another example of MRN participants advocating less speech as they push for more speech on the airwaves.

In an indication that others were following the thread even if they were not actively contributing, Richard Edmondson from San Francisco Liberation Radio responded to Tymon with a gentle rejoinder to ignore threads he doesn't like rather than tell people to stop talking:

The debate may not interest you, but it IS an aspect of micro radio. Suggestion: take an alka seltzer for your headache, click your delete button and move on. (MRN post by Richard Edmondson, July 16, 2000)

Tymon responded to Edmondson, adding detail to his previous post and defending his attempt to protect the MRN from degenerating from a tool for political organization around LPFM to a forum for irrelevant diatribes.

A debate about whether Christians are evil, blessed or somewhere in between is a waste of my time and irrelevant to this list. This IS an issue because if this list becomes irrelevant, many people will drop off it and then our ability to use this list effectively for focused and serious discussion of our strategies and tactics will be lost. And that will be a great lose—I have learned and gained a great deal from this list and have put much of what I've learned into my efforts. (MRN post by Philip Tymon, July 16, 2000)

Edmondson did not agree with the requirement of focused discussion as criteria for an effective list. He responded to Tymon with:

I disagree with you that lively debate (about religion or whatever) inspires people to withdraw from this list. However, since this discussion is causing your mouse finger to feel so aggrieved and put upon, I am quite willing to take this discussion off list. However, I must implore you—please don't deny those of us who obtain daily amusement from The Slave's postings. (MRN post by Richard Edmondson, July 17, 2000)

This post reveals a level of observation on the part of the MRN subscribers. Though the threads may be limited to a few participants, others were watching the development of the discourse and learning from the dialogue.

Another person who watched this discourse unfold was Bob Marston. Bob wrote:

I've been watching this thread for quite a while. You guys have quite a rhubarb going. . . . "Be it left or right, the level of political development in this country is disgraceful," Michael Parenti.

Another point brought out by Parenti and Noam Chomsky is that there is a very sizable and active Christian left in this country. They played a major role in the Santuary Movement that went on around the war in El Salvador. . . . These are the Christians that should be applying for LPFM licenses.

The liberals seem far more content to stop someone else's gig than approach a problem from a constructive vantage point. THAT IS A LOSERS MENTALITY!

The Nation of Islam views the LPFM project as an excellent opportunity to organize their followers. Has anyone looked into contacting the Nation of Islam to see how we could work together?? The opportunity is out there if only people would check their egos and agendas! (MRN post by Bob Marston, July 17, 2000)

Marston's comments integrate ideas from the academic discourse portion of the movement and attempt to place the Christian issue into the larger context of left politics and strategy.

Finally, The Slave responded to Tymon and the call to limit discussion of this topic. The Slave continued to push for discussion and organization within the movement. Just because Christians were a powerful group did not mean the LPFM community should be resigned to religious domination of the new radio service. The Slave wrote:

If you read what I've been posting, it's always come back around to the idea that LPFMers need to come together and hammer out what sort of deal they would like. An agenda of sorts.

Unless the LPFM community starts having national conferences, such as the war council meeting, they will never get what they want. This also means that individual LPFMers need to get a little professional by making sure they come up money to send representatives, etc.

It is an issue of defining priorities yourself . . . or letting someone else define them for you. It is obvious that the NAB is in control of the entire process at this time. Individual LPFMers "just doing their thing" isn't going to change that. They will have to get organized nationally or they will lose. The NAB is just too damned powerful and ahs too much money.

You can't let the FCC and the NAB define the boundaries of the debate. You have to take the bull by the horns and define the shape of LPFM yourselves. (MRN post by The Slave, July 18, 2000)

One interesting feature of The Slave's posts was the use of the third person to describe "LPFMers." Despite his active participation in Free Radio Austin and the MRN list, The Slave distanced himself from the LPFM community. His comments were phrased as encouragement to the micro broadcasters instead of "we" statements. The thread reveals the intricate web of issues embodied in the struggle to define Christians as friend or foe (Other).

The dialogue that took place around this topic also shows how the process of dialogue and discourse formation raises issues of movement strategy and tactics (i.e., boycotts, strategic alliances), distinct from the specific issue itself (i.e., NPR, commercialism, Christians). The listserv discussion reveals the active participation of micro broadcasters and supporters nationwide, exchanging ideas and developing the contours of the cognitive terrain the movement embodied. This terrain was constantly shifting as political and social changes took place. As new groups became interested in micro radio (i.e., Christians), the activists were forced to respond and develop conceptual tools to accommodate the new forces as they emerged. This fluidity is the nature of social movements and is part of the process where the knowledge produced by the movement is integrated into more public and common conceptions of society.

The two issues examined in this chapter, NPR and the Christian community's influence on the micro radio activists, present detailed case study examples of the process of movement formation. The listserv discussions reveal the difficult process of identifying "the Other" and creating strategies for responding to opponents. These listerv exchanges are a historical record of one aspect of movement formation and their summary allows for the tracing of a discourse through the history of a movement as it grew and changed. Both NPR and the Christian community's involvement in the micro radio struggle presented unique and unexpected challenges to the activists. These challenges were met with strong language from a variety of ideological perspectives. As these opinions were shared on-line, dialogue took place that encouraged the activists to look beyond monolithic conceptions of institutions and find the discontinuities that exist and offer opportunities for movement support. By looking for openings for resistance within their opponents, the micro radio community attempted to fragment their opposition in much the same way they accused their opponents of doing to the activist community. NPR affiliates were petitioned to break with the national organization's agenda and local churches were enlisted to support measures that would limit the influence of national Christian broadcasting organizations. Thus a part of the cognitive terrain and cognitive praxis (theory and practice if you will) that was developed by the activists included political strategies for getting their knowledge out into a public forum and for responding to opponents as they emerged. As the next chapter demonstrates, the activists had a measure of success in enlisting the press to aid in the dissemination of the ideas behind micro radio in particular and media activism in general.

4

Representing Micro Radio: Newspaper Coverage of the Micro Radio Issue, 1998–2000

The 1990s was an active period in the development of micro radio theory and practice and the final three years of the decade led to a compelling climax. In the early 1990s, pirate (and later micro) radio gained nominal media attention, largely through the legal cases fought by Stephen Dunifer. As Dunifer's legal case developed and many other prosecuted micro radio operators replicated his legal arguments, press coverage of the micro radio movement grew. With the combination of a new set of FCC rules for licensing micro radio and growing opposition to micro radio from the NAB and NPR, a major story from the media activism and reform movement began to gain traction in local and national newspapers across the country. The news stories from this time period document the positions of key players in this debate and contain indicators about the popular attitude toward a formerly obscure issue. The articles document one form of the public display of discourse and knowledge created by the micro radio community. By examining the newspaper coverage of the micro radio for the three years (1998–2000)—a period of increased action at the grassroots, institutional, academic and governmental levels—a pattern emerges, revealing cultural acceptance for the activists' discourse and the evolution of the cognitive space created by the movement from the periphery to the center.

1998–2000: A SUMMARY OF THE EVENTS

In February 1998, The FCC received two petitions calling for the creation of very small, low-power FM stations. These proposals received little formal attention from the press, although they were acknowledged in a number of articles about micro radio. 1998 was a busy year for the FCC as they enforced regulations and closed down almost 300 illegal micro radio stations. This enforcement included confrontation with the micro broadcasters and was often an impetus for the press coverage during the year.

In 1999 the FCC responded to the citizen-initiated petitions from the previous year. The FCC proposed the licensing of micro radio stations. On January 28, 1999, the FCC issued a "Notice of Proposed Rulemaking" (NPRM) that would legalize low power FM radio stations ranging from 10 to 1,000 watts. This proposal left many questions unanswered. Would the stations be commercial or noncommercial? Would the current illegal broadcasters be eligible for station ownership? Would there be *any* ownership requirements on the new micro stations? How would the FCC resolve competing applications for available frequencies? These and a host of other questions became the source of a protracted debate within the micro radio community. Twice the FCC, at the request of the NAB, extended the initial sixty-day comment period where the public was allowed to submit opinions to these and other questions. The reply comment period, usually ninety days from the initiation of a proposed rule was extended as well. Thus the two comment periods, originally scheduled to end April 12 and May 12, respectively, were extended resulting in comment closing dates of August 2, 1999, and September 1, 1999.

Almost one year after the proposed rule to license micro radio, on January 20, 2000, the FCC issued a "Report and Order" detailing the rules for the new micro radio, low-power FM radio service. This action prompted a relatively positive response from the micro radio community and a very negative response from the NAB. With the regulatory action of the FCC favoring the activists over industry, the NAB turned their attention to the U.S. Congress as they worked to overturn the new LPFM rules. After a number of attempts by members of Congress and a number of different pieces of legislation, the U.S. Congress passed, and President Clinton signed, the Radio Broadcasting Preservation Act of 2000. This severely curtailed the FCC's LPFM rule, reducing the number of possible stations by more than 80% and creating a trial period where stations would be issued licenses subject to review after one year.

This summary of the governmental action affecting micro radio from 1998 to 2000 (see Figure 4.1) provided the context for the analysis of the news coverage that follows. These three years represent an important time in the trajectory of micro radio, a time where the work of many people culminated in a series of actions by the key players in the micro radio debate. The micro radio debate even reached the White House and the 2000 presidential campaign. Thus the cognitive terrain defined through the micro radio discourse was partially absorbed into dominant institutions. The movement of micro radio discourse from the periphery to the center is part of the predicted evolution of the social movement model proposed by Eyerman and Jamison (1991) and indicated a measure of success on the part of the people involved, who helped move LPFM from the housing projects of Springfield, Illinois, into the federal register and the halls of Congress.

Figure 4.1
Micro Radio Timeline: January 1, 1998 to December 31, 2000

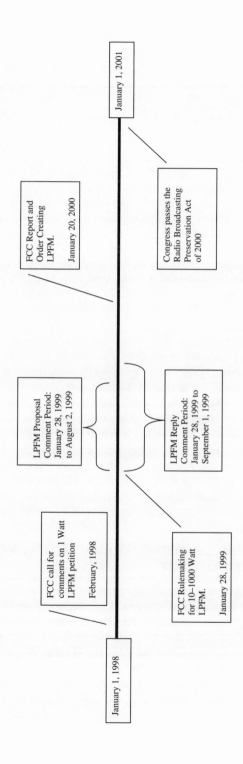

STORY STRUCTURE

Most of the stories across the three years began with a specific, grounded example of one micro radio broadcaster. The person, and the station he or she was affiliated with, was described in relation to government action; closing them down, moving ahead with a proposal that could grant them a license, or enacting new laws limiting the implementation of legal low-power radio. Examples of story leads featuring radio pirates include:

The nerve center of a nationwide and rapidly growing renegade radio broadcasting movement lies here, in the cluttered and dimly lit home of a frail and soft-spoken radio technician. (*Los Angeles Times*, March 5, 1998, p. A1)

The federal government has seized radio equipment at two more locations where it says unlicensed broadcasting was taking place. (*St. Petersburg Times*, April 15, 1998, p. 4B)

Inspired by a growing national microbroadcasting movement and a recent conference on pirate radio, a pair of low-power, unlicensed stations are preparing to start broadcasting to East Harlem and the South Bronx. (*New York Times*, June 7, 1998, sect. 14 p. 6)

The specific activist narrative was usually followed by a summary of the current regulatory situation offered by either an academic from a local university or from a nonprofit media policy group such as the Media Access Project. The policy context would usually include a quote from William Kennard, the chairman of the FCC. Finally, the story would include information from dissenting voices, usually a spokesperson from the NAB and/or NPR.

This story pattern is significant because the information that was included to tell the story of micro radio, as well as who was chosen to tell what pieces of the story, represent a public space in which the movement disseminated its discourse and knowledge. The news stories often contained information from representatives of the three groups described in the media activism typology. The presence of these three groups points to the unique knowledge that each contributed to the movement and shows how that knowledge was pick up and disseminated to a broader public.

FRAMES AND SOURCES: NEWSPAPER COVERAGE OF MICRO RADIO, 1998–2000

In looking at the newspaper coverage of micro radio during this period of significant activity, a number of patterns quickly emerge. The "news" section of the papers contained the most articles about micro radio, followed by the "business" section and the "entertainment" sections. This indicates that the issue of micro radio was largely considered a topic of broad interest and significance, resulting in the placement in the dominant "news" section of the papers. Micro radio was also considered to be a story about "business" and a story about "entertainment." These general categories for the placement of the micro radio struggle are connected to issues within the struggle. As we will see, micro radio is presented as a story of broad social significance, a struggle over money, and a story about access to culture, music and entertainment.

The dominant frame for the news coverage of micro radio from 1998 to 2000 centered on the actions of the illegal broadcasters. The majority of the stories were initiated by the interaction between activists—who were broadcasting illegally—and the FCC who as acting to shut them down. Of the forty articles examined from 1998, thirty-one were focused on the "pirates" and their interactions with the FCC. Headlines from 1998 included:

Pirate Radio Trial Gets Underway. (*Tampa Tribune,* February 25, 1998, p. 4)

Radio Pirates Fight the Power Low-Watt: Illegal Stations Spice Up Corporate Ruled Dial. (*USA Today,* February 27, 1998, p. 1B)

Defiant Pirates Ply the Radio Airwaves. (*Los Angeles Times,* March 5, 1998, p. 1)

Pirates Defend Rights to Airwaves. (*Baltimore Sun,* April 13, 1998, p. 2A)

Yo Ho Ho and a Battle of Broadcasters. (*Washington Post,* October 6, 1998, p. D2)

The civil disobedience of the micro broadcasters, going on the air in defiance of FCC regulations, drew the attention of the FCC and in turn, drew the attention of the media. Although many of these stories could have been a simple tale of law enforcement, these stories focused on the broadcasters, giving them ample room to voice their ideas and opinions. Newspapers rarely give extended coverage to the articulations of people accused of other crimes, (i.e., armed robbery, embezzlement, public drunkenness, etc.) but the micro radio issue was more complex than a simple crime story. Thus the civilly disobedient illegal broadcasting of the micro radio community in some cases gained local media attention, although more often the media attention followed law enforcement actions by the FCC. The ensuing legal struggle became "news" at the local and national level.

As time progressed and the FCC initiated further proposals to license LPFM, the news frame shifted as well. Of the twenty-nine stories and six editorials dealing with micro radio examined from 1999, sixteen of the stories had headlines centered around the FCC and appeared to be initiated by governmental action to license LPFM. Eleven stories followed the dominant frame, documenting the interaction between the FCC and activists. Four of the six editorials examined for 1999 dealt expressly with the new FCC policy proposals. Thus the news frame progressed as the issue expanded to include more than confrontation between the government and activists. As the FCC picked up and promoted the idea of low-power FM (LPFM), the news frame shifted to the struggle over policy. As we know, Congress passed legislation limiting the FCC's authority to license LPFM stations and this intragovernmental struggle came to dominate the newspaper coverage in 2000.

SAMPLES FROM THE MOVEMENT:
GRASSROOTS VOICES

That so many of the stories began with the personal experiences of micro broadcasters points to the power of the practices developed by this disparate group. The act of broadcasting illegally became the starting point for many of the stories about micro radio. This civil disobedience, like other acts of protest such as sit-ins, marches, roadblocks, or other tactics used by a host of social movements, was effective for two reasons. First, the actual practice of micro broadcasting created the opportunity to demonstrate the potential of this technology in terms of both content and logistics. Once on the air, a station could demonstrate meaningful contributions to the local community. Recognition of the contribution of individual stations came in the form of listener support for the stations and from local government awards and citations acknowledging public service. Free Radio Allston was one such station that received a letter of commendation from the Boston City Council.

In addition to demonstrating valuable programming, micro radio stations that went on the air illegally also demonstrated a technical feasibility that was consistently questioned by the NAB. Every station that operated without significant interference supported the argument that there was space in the broadcast spectrum for these new stations to be added. Some stations did cause interference with other radio as well as airplane communication. In most cases though, it was in the micro broadcasters interest to prevent interference because complaints about interference were one of the primary ways the FCC located and shut down micro broadcasters.

Stephen Dunifer, the founder of Free Radio Berkeley, demonstrated the importance of the technical aspects of broadcasting to the promotion of micro radio. By broadcasting in the San Francisco Bay area for more than two years while waging his court battle, Dunifer demonstrated that even in a densely populated city with a crowded radio dial, small-scale local stations could be added without disrupting the existing system.

The power of the sign was the second significant contribution of grassroots micro broadcasting activism. While the act of illegal broadcasting produced programming content and technological practices, this form of protest also took on symbolic value. Micro radio became a sign that the media picked up and used to tell the story. Writing about social movements, Melucci states,

Movements no longer operate as characters but as signs. They do this in the sense that they translate their action into symbolic challenges that upset the dominant cultural codes and reveal their irrationality and partiality by acting at the levels at which the new forms of technocratic power also operate (Melucci, 1989, p. 249).

Thus, the act of micro broadcasting confronted the technocratic rational behind the FCC regulations and created a symbol of resistance that was then re-presented by the newspapers. In the news articles, micro radio became a sign that was imbued with a host of primarily positive connotations. The newspaper coverage shows the influence of the theoretical and practical knowledge created by the micro broadcasters, as well as the newspapers' attempts to articulate the symbolic meaning of the act of illegal broadcasting.

Some basic numbers provide a summary of the media presence of the grassroots activists. One micro broadcaster who received a lot of media attention was Stephen Dunifer, the founder of Free Radio Berkeley. Through his high-profile legal challenges and his active leadership, Dunifer was often identified as a leader of this largely leaderless movement. Of the 129 stories examined, Stephen Dunifer was quoted or referenced in twenty of them, better than 13% of the newspaper coverage. Examples of references to and quotes from Dunifer include:

"I feel very strongly that in the court of public opinion we've already won our case," Dunifer said." You can shut off one radio station, but you can't shut off an idea whose time has come. That idea is democratic grassroots media under the control of average community people." (*The San Francisco Chronicle,* June 16, 1998, p. A27)

"As far as I'm concerned, all avenues of any equitable redress in this country have been cut off to the average person," Dunifer said. "We've exhausted every legal remedy available to us, so therefore the only route that seems effective in achieving our goals will always be direct action and electronic civil disobedience." (*The San Francisco Chronicle,* July 21, 2000, p. A17)

These quotes and descriptions provide some detail about a major figure in the micro radio grassroots community. Dunifer used a variety of discursive concepts in his comments, ranging from "civil disobedience" to issues of media access and democracy. His comments reflect his technical as well as his ideological understanding that contributed to both the knowledge and the skills (or practices) that have emerged out of this movement.

SAMPLES FROM THE MOVEMENT: INSTITUTIONS

The set of newspaper articles examined also offer insight into how the more institutional organizations engaged this social movement. One prominent nonprofit media policy organization was the Media Access Project (MAP). MAP was a public interest telecommunications law firm located in Washington, DC. Founded in 1972, this firm addressed a wide variety of media policy issues and existed before micro radio emerged as an issue. Because of their history and expertise, MAP was an excellent example of an institution that was part of a broad media activism and reform movement, working primarily out of public view until the micro radio issue emerged as an opportunity to present their knowledge to the public within a specific historical and political context.

The directors of MAP, Andrew Schwartzman, and Cheryl Leanza were often included in the news articles about micro radio. Either Schwartzman or Leanza were quoted in twelve of the 129 articles examined. They were supporters of micro radio, though the knowledge and skills they brought to the movement were distinct from those of the grassroots activists. The following references and quotes provide an overview of the discursive contributions this institution made to the specific micro radio debate:

After the 1999 FCC announcement to license LPFM
The proposed change would relax the regulations to allow new broadcasters to transmit in areas from 2 miles to 8.8 miles. There is need all over the country for micro-radio, said Cheryl A. Leanza, a lawyer for the Media Access Project, a nonprofit telecommunications law firm. (*New York Times,* February 22, 1999, p. C9)

On the NAB's motives
Cheryl Leanza of the Media Access Project says the NAB's technical concerns mask worries "that they would have to compete for listeners." (*USA Today,* January 7, 2000, p. 1B)

Attempting to influence Congress
The war is raging in the media, too. The Public Media Center, a San Francisco nonprofit advocacy agency, and the Media Access Project, a Washington, D.C., public-interest law firm, funded recent full-page ads in the *Washington Post,* the *New York Times* and a dozen regional papers. The ads urged consumers to contact the White House, Senate and House to voice their support for opening up the airwaves and accused the broadcasting lobby of trying to keep broadcasting in the hands of a few corporations. (*San Francisco Chronicle,* June 18, 2000, p. 54)

Describing the LPFM applicants
Andrew Jay Schwartzman, president of Media Access Project, an advocacy group, said that while the large number of conservative religious groups applying for licenses surprised some, the fact is that the applicants represent diverse views and philosophies.

"We never thought of low-power radio that split on purely liberal-conservative, left or right, secular or religious groups," he said. "The applicants so far represent scores of demographic niches and interest groups that have gone underserved in the various communities across the country as a result of radio consolidation." (*The Times-Picayune,* September 3, 2000, p. 6)

MAP weighed in on a number of issues, contesting the NAB's interference argument, providing advocacy ads in major newspapers and acknowledging public support for LPFM across the ideological spectrum. Because of their position as lawyers researching public policy, their comments add to the weight of the discourse. Although activists may have been able to make these same points, the fact that lawyers and researchers were affirming the activists position added to the credibility of the discourse. Also, because reporters look to "experts" to verify the accusations of "wild eyed activists," MAP served as an important legitimating force. Also in terms of story structure, reporters look for outside opinions. A news piece would rarely devote an article entirely to activists. When professionals working within existing institutions support a movement, they are likely to be added to activist quotes, not substituted for them. Thus a wide range of voices supporting micro radio was included, occupying more space on the page and adding public credibility to the micro radio discourse.

The newsroom practice of relying on established, credible sources has been noted by other scholars (Shoemaker & Reese, 1991). The lawyers at MAP and representatives from other institutions such as the American Civil Liberties Union (ACLU) or the United Church of Christ (UCC) were familiar, trusted sources reporters often turned to for information on short notice: "Not all sources are equally likely to be contacted by journalists—those with economic and political power are more likely to influence news reports than those who lack power" (Shoemaker & Reese, 1991, p. 151). The "institutions" involved in the media activism movement played a critical role by providing grounded, trusted information to the news media. That information was often the same set of facts and ideas that the activists promoted but it was the institutional credibility in the eyes of the newsroom that led to their consistent citation by the newspapers and thus public support of micro radio.

SAMPLES FROM THE MOVEMENT: ACADEMIC DISCOURSES

Like the institutional voices that weighed in on the micro radio debate, academic scholars were often used in the news articles to add perspective to the micro radio debate. These professors play a significant role in researching issues that may not have direct policy applications but still influence the way we think about our social world. Clearly not all academic discourses come from, or are connected to, university professors, though most academic discourses pass through universities in one form or another. Thus the presence of university researchers in these news articles revealed participation of the third piece of the activism typology in the process of connecting movement knowledge and practices of the movement with a larger public audience.

Of the 129 articles examined, eleven cited professors in the portrayal of the micro radio debate. The following quotes and representations provide a summary of the kinds of contributions these people made to the public presentation of the movement discourse.

On the effects of media concentration
This [media consolidation] trend has taken radio out of the mom-and-pop operation, ushering in a new era of corporate ownership, cost-cutting and centralized programming. And that has meant the death of local news coverage, public service programs and other locally generated shows, said Robert McChesney, an associate professor of journalism at the University of Wisconsin. "The electronic medium that should be the most decentralized and the most open to local access and local ownership is becoming the most centralized and has the least access of any medium," McChesney said. (*The Times-Picayune,* July 12, 1998, p. A30)

Contributing technical knowledge
The NAB claims that signal and static "bleed" from the low-power stations will harm their listenership. That claim is flatly contradicted by studies like the one that Ted Rappaport, an electrical engineering professor at Virginia Tech and leading authority on signal interference, presented to Congress last month. Rappaport said that "in the absolute worst case" only 1.6% of the micro-radio stations would bleed into existing station signals. (*Los Angeles Times,*

March 27, 2000, p. 4B)

On the history of broadcast law
The debate is particularly important, low-power advocates say, because of radio's historical mission. When the government first established rules for television and radio broadcasters earlier in the century, it limited the number of national networks in order to set aside a large part of the spectrum for local broadcasters. That decision, said Akhil Reed Amar, a professor at Yale Law School, had its roots in the founders' desire to stitch a number of smaller democracies into a large one. (*New York Times,* July 16, 2000, Section 4, p. 4)

With these passages, we see academic scholars contributing critical perspectives, technical knowledge and legal history. These wider perspectives support the micro radio issue, though from a position legitimized by universities. These are examples of the way academic discourses became integrated into the media activism and reform movement and served to advance the ideas within the movement through the contribution of credible, specialized knowledge.

The three previous sections, "Grassroots Voices," "Institutions," and "Academic Discourses" provide a glimpse of the way major newspapers presented various pieces of the micro radio movement. There were many other contributions to the micro radio discourse in the news articles examined; more grassroots activists quoted, other institutional voices presented and other scholars as well. The quotations were intended as examples, representatives of the types of information that came from each of the three groups in the media activism typology. The examples chosen were from people who made significant contributions to the movement. Other voices and perspectives will emerge throughout this chapter. This section was merely intended to identify a few of the key players within the movement and provide examples of the type of contribution each general category of participant makes to the larger social project.

METAPHORS: ROSA PARKS AND
DAVID AND GOLIATH

Another way to examine the newspaper coverage of the micro radio movement is to look at the metaphors that were used to describe the movement. Sometimes the activists themselves, attempting to invoke particular associations, used these metaphors and in other cases reporters used images to develop the themes embodied in the micro radio struggle. Two metaphors emerged that warrant attention because of the images they promote and the connections they make with previous social struggles: Rosa Parks and David and Goliath.

In their argument about the connections between social movements, Eyerman and Jamison (1991) contend that successive social movements build on those of the past, learning from, refining, and experimenting with previous strategies for advancing a cause:

Both feminism and environmentalism are inconceivable without the student movement of the 1960s. Their reconceptualizations of nature and gender, and of social relations more generally, were impossible without the articulation of a more fundamental belief in liberation. (Eyerman & Jamison, 1991, p. 91)

In the case of micro radio, activists experimented with varieties of civil disobedience as a way to gain attention while making a political statement. The primary form this took was illegal broadcasting. The metaphor of Rosa Parks appeared in a number of articles and was apt in many ways, linking the present struggle to previous movements for justice and equity. In an article following the FCC announcement of the LPFM licensing rules, *The San Francisco Examiner* ran a story describing the new rules:

The ruling bans current and past pirate radio operators from applying for 10 years unless they closed down after being ordered to do so by the FCC.

Many of these radio operators were leaders in the fight that led to the FCC ruling.

"This was a civil disobedience movement," said Peter Franck of the National Lawyers Guild's Committee on Democratic Communication, which has been waging the legal battle for micro-radio stations. "It's like saying Rosa Parks is the only one who can't sit in the front of the bus." (*The San Francisco Examiner,* January 24, 2000, p. C1)

Though the FCC moved ahead with a plan to license micro radio, the people who were most responsible for advancing the issues behind the technology were set up to be the last ones to benefit from the policy. Thus the metaphor (or simile in this case) of micro broadcasters as similar to Rosa Parks made the connection with the previous work of the civil rights movement. Peter Franck was a lawyer who had been involved with micro radio since the Kantako case in the late 1980s. His quote in this article was another indication of the presence of the various components of the Media Activism and Reform Movement. As a civil rights lawyer who spent part of his time on the micro radio issue, he represented an institutional voice within the movement, a voice that worked within established power structures applying his knowledge of law in the service of the movement.

Another member of the micro radio community repeated the Rosa Parks metaphor. In this second example, the activist was an illegal broadcaster. This quote revealed a level of communication within the community and between the categories outlined in the movement typology.

Jerry Szoka became Cleveland's best-known micro broadcaster in four years of operating unlicensed GRID FM/96.9.

GRID, which played commercial-free dance music and a talk show aimed at the gay community, ceased operation in February after U.S. District Judge Kathleen O'Malley granted the FCC a permanent injunction.

One of the (new LPFM) rules would disqualify him from a license, since he operated in violation of an FCC cease-and-desist order.

"I did it in a responsible way," he said. "But they're penalizing people who brought the issue to the table. To bar microradio pioneers from the airwaves is equivalent to continuing to require Rosa Parks to ride in the back of the bus.

"The radio spectrum, which we the public own, is being monopolized by just a few people, big corporations who are filling the pockets of Congress." (*The Plain Dealer,* April 20, 2000, p. 1E)

Thus the link is made again. Although the struggles may contain many similar issues, a close examination of the comparison of media activists to African Americans and their struggle for equal voting, education and opportunity rights may lack balance for some. The comparison may be limited, but the similarity lies with the people who broke laws to make a political statement. The lunch counter sit-in protesters were not denied access once lunch counters were desegregated and the micro radio activists hoped to be allowed to benefit from the work they had done promoting the LPFM issue.

A second metaphor that appeared a number of times was the image of David and Goliath. Unlike the previous metaphor, which was used by the activists to describe themselves, this biblical reference was used by the reporters writing the newspaper articles. In a 1998 article from *USA Today,* the micro broadcasters don't even rise to the level of David:

From dining rooms, basements, garages and even car batteries across the nation, these guerrilla broadcasters beam their illicit FM signals at under 100 watts. They are mere flyspecks compared with the 3,000- to 100,000-watt commercial FM goliaths that blanket entire regions. (*USA Today,* February 27, 1998, p. 1B)

In this case, the micro broadcasters were "mere flyspecks" while the commercial broadcasters were the "goliaths" that dominate the airwaves yet remain vulnerable to their smaller opposition. As the biblical story goes, it was the small boy David who brought down the powerful giant Goliath. Given the commercial broadcasters' wealth and dominance of the airwaves, it is easy to assume they are the goliath in the analogy, although not everyone agreed with this assumption.

The battle over low-power FM has been characterized on both sides as David vs. Goliath. But, grumbles NAB communications director Dennis Wharton, "who's David and who's Goliath?"

Indeed, the low-power advocates have assembled a mighty lobby, taking full advantage of today's technology—e-mail and Web sites—to spread the gospel.

The NAB responded with battle tactics of its own, calling on its longtime relations with members of Congress. (*Washington Post,* January 20, 2000, p. C1)

Here the NAB attempted to invert the metaphor, positioning themselves as the embattled "David" struggling against the public wielding the tools of the Internet and civil disobedience. The fact that the NAB even felt threatened by the micro radio activists was an indication of the effectiveness of the knowledge and practices developed by the movement. A member of the activist community noted this point in the same article.

"This demonstrates that, in the advocacy fight, the Internet and e-mail are forever changing lobbying," says Michael Bracy, a Washington lawyer who is the executive director of the Low Power Radio Coalition, the clearinghouse for low-power advocates. "This would have been a slam-dunk for the NAB five years ago." (*Washington Post,* January 20, 2000, p. C1)

This quote emphasized the impact of the digital technology on the power of organization. The media activism and reform movement was influenced by, and had connections to, the lessons of previous social movements; employing strategies of civil disobedience and at the same time exploring new avenues for coordinating action and information.

As the micro radio issue moved from a struggle between activists and the FCC into a struggle between the FCC and Congress, the metaphor was reapplied.

This story, looking at first blush like a David vs. Goliath tale, turns out to be something else—a classic Washington power struggle of political Olympians clashing miles above Huron's head [Amanda Huron was an activist from Washington, DC]. (*Washington Post,* May 15, 2000, p. A1)

Though the micro broadcasters (David) had made a significant impact on the commercial broadcasters (Goliath) and the FCC, in the end they were not able to stop a larger political struggle from playing out. It can be argued that they prompted the "clashing of the Olympians," forcing the NAB to turn to Congress when the FCC had initiated action to support micro radio.

These metaphors were a small part of the representation of the micro radio discourse that appeared in the newspaper coverage. The images and associations they evoke tell us something about this social struggle and what was at stake. Connecting micro radio to Rosa Parks served to remind the reader of the history of social struggle for equity and justice, and placed the "pirates" in the ranks of social heroes like Parks who stood up (or sat down as the case may be) for what she believed in. Similarly, the association with David and Goliath invoked the age-old image of the small, everyday person struggling against the powerful giant. With this image, the micro broadcasters were given the symbolic power to actually kill commercial broadcasters. Relying on small radio signals, little money and marginal political clout, micro radio posed a very real threat to an industry dominated by a few enormous media conglomerates.

REPRESENTING KENNARD: PROSECUTOR, PROMOTER, OR SELF-PROMOTER?

William Kennard, the chairman of the FCC, played a significant role during this three-year struggle over micro radio. Depending on one's vantage point, he was a vigilant law enforcer, a champion of the people, or a reckless administrator dead set on disrupting the broadcast industry. In addition to using Kennard's own words, the media picked up many of the comments and criticism about Kennard as they portrayed this key player in the micro radio debate. As chairman of the FCC, Kennard played a powerful discursive role in this issue and the power of his words was often a source of contention for both the advocates and the opponents of micro radio.

As the first African American to head the FCC, William Kennard hoped to integrate his commitment to social justice with his leadership on broadcast policy. His biography on the FCC's web site states,

Bill Kennard is committed to making sure that all Americans—no matter where they live, what their age, or what special needs they may have—have access to the technologies that are driving our economy and shaping our society.

Kennard has been called, "a consumer advocate for the digital age," fighting to protect consumers in the telecom marketplace and ensuring that they have the information needed to make the best choices for them in a competitive marketplace. (www.fcc.gov., accessed June 5, 2001)

This commitment to "all Americans" proved difficult to implement in an agency known for its commitment to the broadcast industry. Beginning his term as chairman in November 1997, shortly after his first year and the 1998 elections, Kennard was promoting the idea of free airtime to presidential candidates. Concerned about the $500 million spent by candidates on television commercials in 1998, Kennard proposed that television broadcasters be required to provide free airtime to candidates. This idea was quickly withdrawn after the NAB pressured Congress and Congress in turn threatened to hold full hearings on the continued existence of the FCC (McChesney, 1999). Congress issued a similar threat after Kennard proposed rolling back the deregulation that had allowed the massive consolidation in the broadcast industry (McChesney, 1999). These early struggles between Congress and Kennard presage the struggle over micro radio. These two conflicts also demonstrate a commitment to consumer advocacy on the part of Kennard and help to explain his eventual support and advocacy for LPFM.

During 1998, prior to the FCC decision to propose licensing LPFM, the quotes chosen to represent Kennard indicated his attempt to balance law enforcement with an acknowledgement of the issues raised by the micro broadcasters. At this stage, the FCC had been engaged in legal struggles with Dunifer and others for a number of years, and they were well aware of the activists' discourse. A *Los Angeles Times* story from 1998 demonstrates this point:

"We have a situation where people are creating confusion and cacophony over the airwaves, we just can't have it," Kennard says. . . . Kennard concedes that micro-broadcasters have a point when they complain that it is hard for community broadcasters to get on the air. "Someone like Stephen Dunifer is doing an unlawful thing," he said. "But I am sympathetic for the need to have more expression on the airwaves. That is a compelling point that some

of these pirates make. We just want them to work in a lawful way to change the system."
(*Los Angeles Times,* March 5, 1998, p. A1)

The recognition of the activists' discourse pointed to their success in moving a peripheral issue into the discourse of the policy arena. For Eyerman and Jamison (1991), this is the classic function of a social movement; challenging "dominant assumptions of the social order" and "putting new issues on the historical agenda." While Kennard enforced existing law he was also able to use the discourse, generated largely by the activists, to advance ideas that confronted consolidation and homogenization in the broadcasting industry. This news article included Kennard's comments about the micro radio movement:

Kennard says he thinks micro-broadcasting has exploded in popularity in the last five years as a backlash against the consolidation of station ownership spurred by the 1996 federal communications law. The movement, he says, has been fed by the Internet. "The Internet has created a way for them to communicate with one another in ways that are pretty powerful, " he says. "They are able . . . to learn how to become a pirate." (*Los Angeles Times,* March 5, 1998, p. A1)

With this, Kennard picked up the micro radio critique of the current broadcasting arrangement. This critique and the cover it provided Kennard as he moved to legitimize LPFM did not originate with micro radio broadcasters, though it was as a result of their practices (specifically, illegal broadcasting) that the idea was moved from the realm of institutional and academic policy discourse into a public arena. Once in the public arena, Kennard used this "backlash against consolidation" theme repeatedly as he deflected criticism and supported licensed micro radio.

The year 1998 was full of contradictions for the FCC with regard to micro radio. In February, the FCC began soliciting public comments in response to a petition to initiate rulemaking procedures for licensing LPFM. At the same time, the FCC was aggressively shutting down illegal broadcasters, using tactics some considered extreme. In an article about a micro radio conference, activists' reactions to recent FCC station closures were quoted.

"FCC Thugs Back Off". . . . The air was thick with accusations of "goon-squad tactics" and "SWAT-type raids" on the part of the agency. . . . 22-year old Kelly Benjamin (radio name: Kelly Kombat) decried the raids. "They handcuffed and hog-tied people," he said. "All we were doing was operating a radio station."

The argument that low-wattage radio is necessary to bring more diversity to the dial seems to be causing some soul searching at the FCC. Commission Chairman William Kennard has called for full enforcement of licensing regulations but has also expressed concern that media mergers have limited the broadcast outlets available to the public. (*The Baltimore Sun,* April 13, 1998, p. 2A)

Kennard was positioned as being on the receiving end of the micro radio discourse, responding to protest as opposed to initiating new policy. Although his background as a community radio DJ while an undergraduate at Stanford was noted in a few articles, the majority of the pieces placed the activists at the center of the production of micro radio discourse. The twin roles of Kennard in 1998, as enforcer and advocate, continued in a *New York Times* piece in August:

"If the FCC truly supported free speech, they would be doing everything in their power to make microradio happen," M. Edmondson, 45, of San Francisco Liberation Radio, said. "Instead they're trying to stamp it out."

In fact, in a new twist in the labored debate over the fate of tiny community radio stations, the FCC appears to be doing both. It is at once aggressively pursuing and shutting down micro stations, while it also considers licensing radio stations that broadcast below 100 watts of power, compared with 50,000 watts for typical radio stations.

"With consolidation, radio has become the province of multi-billion dollar corporations," Mr. Kennard said. "The loss of small religious stations and local programming is very unfortunate."

Mr. Kennard said there was nothing inconsistent in his efforts to crack down on unlicensed stations and to find room for low power stations on the dial. "If there's not some discipline to this process, the spectrum won't work," he said. "We can't have pirates just signing onto frequencies as they chose and broadcasting willy-nilly on the airwaves." (*New York Times,* August 20, 1989, p. G7)

Thus the *New York Times* portrayed Kennard as safeguarding the integrity of the broadcast spectrum while attempting to increase the diversity of the airwaves. Although it was the action of the pirates that initiated the media coverage and the ensuing public dialogue, Kennard was able to separate the FCC from the pirates as he picked up substantive pieces of the pirate's discourse.

As 1998 drew to a close, a year of record micro station closures by the FCC, the news coverage shifted to a focus on an emerging plan to license micro radio. The biggest proponent behind this plan was William Kennard.

It appears the pirates have found a sympathetic—and seemingly improbable—ear in Washington, a kindred spirit of sorts who is in a position to get things done.

He is William E. Kennard, chairman of the FCC and a vocal proponent of licensing "microradio." If Kennard gets his way, scanning the FM dial will once again bring specialized niche broadcasts into the nation's homes, cars and offices.

"There are a lot of people who want to find ways to speak to their communities, and these are not just big corporations that can afford to buy radio stations," Kennard said. "These are churches and schools and small businesses and community based organizations."

Kennard is concerned about "the homogenization of radio around the country." He added, "Remember, it belongs to all of us; it doesn't just belong to a few people who can afford to get into it." (*The Tampa Tribune,* December 30, 1998, p. 1)

While Kennard continued to reference "churches and schools," the micro broadcasters the FCC shut down included Christian patriot advocates and leftist social justice supporters. This article documented Kennard's use of the micro radio discourse. From the legal arguments in the Dunifer case to statements to the press, the micro radio community consistently referred to the cost of accessing radio as a medium of communication as well as the idea that the airwaves were a public resource that was managed by the FCC in the "public interest." Kennard reiterated these ideas while he repudiated the people who had raised the issue up out of the corridors of regulatory agencies and pages of policy journals. The *Tribune* article went on to state:

Kennard is not too concerned about the pirates' opinions and he denies their assertions that their movement pressed him to support microradio. He said he has been interested in equity issues throughout his nearly 20-year career as a communications lawyer.

"I have no interest in protecting pirates or doing anything for them, because they violated the law," he said. "This is for people who want to act responsibly and lawfully and want to come to the FCC and get a license and use it to serve their communities." (*The Tampa Tribune*, December 30, 1998, p. 1)

Thus, Kennard made an active effort to separate himself from the activists at the same time that he repeated many pieces of their discourse and moved to address many of their concerns. This may have been a conscious attempt to insulate himself, the FCC, and the micro radio policy proposal from the assault that lay ahead. The NAB was not going to accept any new stations on the FM dial and they went after Kennard as well as his policies.

With the announcement of the new micro rules in January 1999, the NAB enlisted the help of Congress to prevent their implementation. On February 22, 1999, the *New York Daily News* ran a story with the first indication of this alliance.

The National Association of Broadcasters does not care for the idea (LPFM) at all, fearing audio interference with established stations. Rep. Bill Tauzin (R.-La.), chairman of the House Telecommuncations subcommittee, last week backed the NAB, warning of "staggering ramifications" and asking the FCC to drop the issue altogether. (*New York Daily News,* February 22, 1999, p. 74)

In spite of more than 13,000 requests for licenses to operate micro radio stations from groups and individuals in the two years leading up to the FCC LPFM decision, as well as more than 3,000 public comments submitted to the FCC, the vast majority of which were in support of the FCC licensing scheme, a member of Congress asked the FCC to stop its support for micro radio. Although both Kennard and Congressman Tauzin might have agreed on the "staggering ramifications" of LPFM, their visions of these ramifications could not have been further apart.

The tension between Congress and the FCC continued, evidenced by a *USA Today* article published one month later bearing the headline, "FCC Faces Critics in Congress":

The House telecommunications subcommittee is expected to grill the five FCC commissioners, particularly on what critics consider a penchant to overstep their mandate.

"We're not talking about just tweaking" the agency, says Ken Johnson, a spokesman for subcommittee Chairman Billy Tauzin, R-La. "We want to rein in a lot of its assumed authority." (*USA Today,* March 17, 1999, p. 3B)

This issue proved divisive for Congress. After the subcommittee hearing, Kennard supporters wrote the chairman to support the FCC's decision to move ahead with LPFM. In their letter, they wrote,

The tremendous public demand for micro radio is demonstrated by the proliferation of illegal radio stations, whose operators broadcast at the risk of financial losses and, in some cases, imprisonment. (*Kansas City Star,* May 25, 1999, p. A1)

The role of the grassroots activists was highlighted here, drawing the attention of congressional representatives and serving as an indication that something was amiss in radio land. Although academics and institutional researchers had addressed this issue in other forms, it was the practices of the pirates that gained the attention of these congressmen (and the news media) and helped to motivate their defense of Kennard and the LPFM policy.

The NAB and Tauzin made a concerted effort to portray Kennard and the FCC as moving too quickly and failing to safeguard existing broadcasters. Another strategy used to discredit the policy was to expose the possibility of micro radio's use by racists.

"We do not want to deny schools, churches and civic organizations a voice on the airwaves, but we are not particularly excited about giving the David Dukes of the world a platform either." Said Ken Johnson, spokesman for Billy Tauzin, a republican from Louisiana.

"It's a huge policy decision," Tauzin aide Johnson said.

"Billy told Kennard in no uncertain terms that he is not to proceed with microstations without consulting Congress." (*Kansas City Star,* May 25, 1999, p. A1)

Thus the chairman of the FCC had a policy not only questioned by Congress, but threatened with intervention prior to any congressional vote about the matter. Even before the first license was issued, micro radio was causing upheaval in the policy formation process. Throughout 1999 the media focused on this struggle within the government, largely leaving the activists out of the story.

In an extended piece in the *Los Angeles Times,* the struggle between Kennard and the NAB was given considerable attention. The NAB continued to accuse the FCC of increasing interference for existing stations. Kennard addressed this argument in a speech to the NAB, quoted in the *Los Angeles Times.*

"Frankly, it is not helpful to hear only rhetoric that 'the sky is falling.' " Kennard told the association in a speech before its annual convention in April. "It only serves to undermine the credibility of your arguments in the end." Kennard says later that he understands, but dismisses, the crowded-airwaves argument. "The NAB's approach is to put as few stations out there as possible. My approach is to put as many out there as can be accommodated without creating interference. The airwaves are a public resource and we ought to maximize their use. (*Los Angeles Times, Los Angeles Times Magazine,* June 13, 1999, p. 24)

The article continued with a sympathetic tone toward Kennard as it attempted to represent the response of the NAB.

His argument is reasoned and delivered in even tones—he hardly sounds like a zealot, as one trade journal described him as "The Man Who Killed Radio."

"It's clear that Kennard is totally 100% committed to this and will go to the wall for this one," one insider says. "There clearly is an agenda that the chairman has," a broadcaster adds. (*Los Angeles Times Magazine,* June 13, 1999, p. 24)

This article also revealed that the NAB was not the only group opposing Kennard. In spite of his articulate defense of micro radio and the need to diversify the airwaves, his motives were suspect by some in the micro radio community.

Yet not everyone has a place in Kennard's utopian future. Pirates like Dunifer and Gerry, who have ignored the government's broadcast regulations, will probably be denied licenses under the FCC's "character clause." As a result, many unlicensed broadcasters dismiss the FCC's motives as less than genuine. The commission's real intention, they say, is to co-opt the micro radio movement by dividing it into good and bad broadcasters, rewarding the first group and creating pariahs of the second. Worse, they believe the government will turn low power stations into tiny commercial outlets, beholden to the same financial considerations that homogenized mainstream radio. (*Los Angeles Times, Los Angeles Times Magazine,* June 13, 1999, p. 24)

Thus we see Kennard as a disputed figure, questioned from all sides as he attempted to respond to the public and political pressures. His quotes revealed significant overlap with the discourse of the micro radio advocates; need for diversity, cost of access, public ownership of the airwaves. Nevertheless, the activist community remained skeptical of Kennard, fearful of being "co-opted." As the fight over micro radio moved from the airwaves and into the halls of government, the media designated Kennard the spokesmen for micro radio. Despite the fact that many micro radio activists were dissatisfied with the FCC policy, Kennard's defenses of the FCC proposal became the dominant discourse in support of micro radio.

The tension between the realized goals of a social movement and the idea that once institutionalized, the goals become co-opted, adds a bit of complexity to the evanescent, temporal conception of social movements. Some argue that social movements are successful when they have passed away, the effects of their knowledge production having been integrated into more formal social institutions (Eyerman & Jamison, 1991). The idea of co-opted micro radio points to the actual *process* of integrating a movement's cognitive space as another site of struggle, where superficial pieces of a movement's knowledge and practices may be appropriated without achieving the larger goals of the movement.

The environmental movement has seen its knowledge co-opted in the form of "green washing," where corporations attempt to position products as environmentally friendly while essentially reproducing unsustainable consumer culture. In the case of micro radio, activists were leery of "micro washing," where small was equated with good, even if was commercial, not local, and part of a media conglomerate. Certainly the publishing industry has fallen victim to this model as independent weeklies across the country are now owned and operated by fewer companies. Creative Loafing is an example of this consolidation, publishing weeklies in six major cities in the Southeast. (www.creativeloafing.com). The process of integrating the knowledge generated by a social movement is a contested process, subject to the social forces that inspired the movement in the first instance.

When the FCC voted on the "Report and Order" for the creation of low-power FM radio service on January 20, 2000, many of the advocate's fears were assuaged. The order outlined rules limiting ownership to one station per owner, local residency requirements and noncommercial status for all LPFM stations. This ruling drew instant opposition from the NAB, with many newspapers coving the controversy:

NAB President Edward Fritz issued a terse statement in response to the vote: "The FCC has turned its back on spectrum integrity. Every legitimate scientific study validates that interference will result from [low-power FM]. This FCC has chosen advancement of social engineering over spectrum integrity. It's a sad day for radio listeners." (*The Washington Post*, January 21, 2000, p. E02)

The NAB relied on the issue of interference in most of its statements in opposition to LPFM, claiming the physics of the spectrum could not be altered to include more stations without interference. The January 21 statement accused the FCC of "social engineering," masking the fact that broadcast policy was littered with concepts (public interest, localism, etc.) that attempted to balance first amendment rights with spectrum scarcity. What Fritz argued was that the NAB preferred social engineering that privileged larger stations that occupy larger pieces of the broadcast spectrum. This argument can be seen as naturalizing the current regulatory scheme and making any changes to that "unnatural" and potentially dangerous to radio, as we know it.

The struggle between Kennard and the NAB continued as Congress drafted legislation to limit the implementation of LPFM. Kennard defended the new policy and the technical issues within it. He aggressively defended the FCC and its long history of broadcast regulation while questioning how Congress or the NAB could possibly be better positioned to create broadcast policy. The *New York Times* gave Kennard plenty of space to make his case:

"This is not rocket science. We have studied the way FM signals propagate around the country. The interference argument is being used as a smokescreen to mask the historical battle by incumbents who want to protect their markets," Kennard said.

"The FCC has turned it's back on its principle mission of maintaining spectrum integrity," said Edward O. Fritz, president of the National Association of Broadcasters. "The technical arguments are not a smokescreen. They stand on their own merit. If this could be done, it would have been done 20 years ago." (*New York Times*, March 27, 2000, p. C1)

As the war of words played out in the media, the NAB successfully enlisted the help of NPR in its opposition to LPFM. NPR, like the NAB, was concerned about interference, loss of audience and the possibility that micro stations might encroach on existing FM translators, devices that boost FM signals into rural areas or areas where reception is isolated by mountains. When the U.S. Congress passed legislation limiting the implementation of LPFM and requiring further technical study, Kennard spoke out and again the *New York Times* covered his speech.

"This is very cynical legislation," said William E. Kennard, the chairman of the FCC who first proposed the plan more than a year ago. "As a practical matter it would kill low power FM."

"The FCC has moved without any consideration of the facts," said Representative John Dingell, Democrat of Michigan. "This is a reasonable common sense compromise. It will protect the broadcasters, it will protect the licensees, and above all else, it will protect listeners of the FM spectrum." (*New York Times*, April 14, 2000, p. C1)

This debate raged back and forth throughout 2000 as Congress remained active in the dispute. Kennard consistently defended the policy, reiterating the need for increased diversity and community voices on the radio and the NAB and NPR consistently repeated their concerns about the effect of interference on existing stations and listeners.

"The FCC wanted to add everything but the kitchen sink into the nation's FM radio spectrum, creating significant interference with existing stations and services," Oxley (R-OH) said.

"I don't know what's fuzzier, said Eddie Fritz, NAB president, "The static that comes from low power FM or the FCC's thinking on the issue."

FCC Chairman Kennard saw it differently after the House passed the Oxley bill.

"Special interests triumphed over community interests," he said. "What this is about is fear of new entrants into the market. It is no different from the battles to kill low-power TV, cable TV, satellite radio, and satellite television." (*The Plain Dealer*, April 20, 2000, p. 1E)

Exchanges such as this were common throughout the news stories during the year 2000. The NAB attempted to portray Kennard as a self-promoter who was willing to risk chaos on the FM dial in order to leave his mark on history. By 2000, the activists had softened their criticisms of Kennard, no longer portraying him as a vengeful prosecutor instead, echoing his words of support. Thus, the newspaper representations of Kennard moved from that of tough radio cop to people's advocate in the fight against big business. The NAB attempted to portray him as overzealous in his quest for public access to the airwaves, though the media consistently gave more space to Kennard's defense of his policy than to the NAB repeated accusations of interference.

After the protracted presidential election was finally resolved through a U.S. Supreme Court intervention, the U.S. Congress attached the Radio Broadcasting Preservation Act of 2000 to a major appropriations bill. This strategy was chosen because of President Clinton's expressed support for LPFM and vow to veto the radio preservation act. After passage through the Congress and on its way to the president's desk, the now-familiar positions on this issue received one more round of coverage. The *New York Times* described the radio preservation act as:

The first time in recent memory that lawmakers actually stripped the agency of the power to manage an important part of the spectrum. . . . Mr. Kennard saw this as the cornerstone of his agenda to promote civil-rights issues at the FCC.

Mr. Kennard said the legislation "shows the dangers of politicizing spectrum management."

"This is a resource that everyone has to share," Mr. Kennard said. "We can't allow people who have the spectrum to use their political clout to shut out voices that don't have the same clout. This highlights the power of incumbency. Companies that have spectrum guard it jealously, and they can use Congress to prevent new voices from having access to the airwaves." (*New York Times*, December 19, 2000, p. A1)

And with a predictable response, Fritts was quoted as saying the NAB was: "pleased that Congress has protected radio listeners against additional interference that would have been caused by the FCC low-power initiative" (*New York Times*, December 19, 2000, p. A1). The Radio Broadcasting Preservation Act of 2000 was signed into law the next day. Nevertheless, the FCC proceeded with the licensing of the first 255 stations in twenty states. These stations complied with the more restrictive spectrum spacing imposed by the act and the *New York Times* reported that the 255 stations were less than half of what the initial FCC proposal would have allowed. The majority of the licenses went to churches and schools (*New York Times*, December 22, 2000, p. C5). Most of the approved stations were in rural areas where the radio spectrum is not overly cluttered.

This was hardly the end of the policy, however as President Bush took office, Kennard resigned and was replaced by commissioner Michael Powell. The LPFM application and licensing process continued under the more restrictive guidelines set by Congress. The policy remained in play within the FCC and the micro radio community remained active despite the legislative setbacks.

EDITORIALS

This study examined eighteen newspaper articles that appeared in the editorial section of the papers during the three years 1998–2000. Of those articles, six were policy position editorials written by the newspaper's editorial staff. The other articles were letters to the editor or commentary pieces submitted by other authors. The six editorials written by the newspaper staff were significant because they represented a measure of the degree to which the discourse of the micro radio advocates was adopted or discarded by major newspapers, a social institution that contributes to public discourse. As a force in shaping public opinion, newspapers and the positions they advocate or discourage influence the language and ideas (memes if you will) we think and talk about at any given time. Newspapers are constitutive of historical context, influencing and influenced by the procession of issues and ideas a society confronts. Examining the editorial positions advocated by the major newspapers during this struggle over micro radio is one way of tracing the movement of the cognitive terrain established by the media activism and reform movement from the movement periphery toward the center of social and institutional life.

All of the six pieces written by newspaper editorial staff appeared in the year 2000. This was the year the FCC moved to license LPFM as well as the year Congress passed a law severely limiting the new LPFM licenses. All six of these editorials supported the FCC's plan to license LPFM. The first piece appeared about two weeks after the FCC's announcement of the new LPFM rules. The *Denver Rocky Mountain News* wrote:

The FCC admits it doesn't quite know where the micro radio movement is headed, but it's good that the regulatory agency is willing to give it a chance. The hope is that small stations will be an outlet for off-brand and offbeat music, politics and local voices that have been left behind in the consolidation of big radio. (*Denver Rocky Mountain News,* February 6, 2000, p. 2B)

The discourse of consolidation was picked up in this piece, as was the idea that there was a "movement" pushing the issue of micro radio. This editorial acknowledged the importance of the movement in bringing micro radio onto the national policy agenda and encouraged the FCC to reward the activists who had worked to promote micro radio:

The FCC is ambiguous about licensing existing pirate stations, but these are the operations most dedicated to the concept and they deserve a regulatory break. The FCC has an essential role in ensuring clear broadcast signals but it also has an essential role in seeing that there are radio bands for as many voices as possible—including the pirates. (*Denver Rocky Mountain News,* February 6, 2000, p. 2B)

The *Rocky Mountain News* acknowledged the NAB's interference argument, although also emphasized the need for diversity on the airwaves. Thus, the content diversity discourse as well as amnesty for pirate broadcasters was supported by this newspaper, both of which were significant parts of the micro radio discourse.

The second editorial regarding micro radio appeared in the *Washington Post*. It published three of the six editorials, possibly because of their proximity to the government struggling to make sense of micro radio. The *Post* summarized the issue by saying:

The idea is to give access to the airwaves to those who don't have any. Since the low power stations will be non-commercial broadcasters using signal strengths of only a small fraction of the power of commercial radio, it doesn't seem like much of a threat. Yet an immense lobbying effort has begun to stop the commission in its tracks. (*Washington Post*, March 30, 2000, p. 20)

The focus of this piece was on the struggle between the FCC and the commercial broadcasters with little mention of the micro radio advocates. The editorial placed the FCC as the active agent promoting LPFM and questioned the motives of industry's opposition to the new policy. Noting the war of "studies," where NAB data pointed to the increased likelihood of interference from low-power stations while FCC data suggested otherwise, the *Post* came down on the side of the FCC.

The commission's studies seem both more persuasive technically and less self-interested. . . . If low-power radio causes problems, the agency will be politically accountable. But if the FCC—the agency charged with protecting the integrity of the spectrum—is persuaded that micro-radio will not cause difficulties, this potentially useful area should be allowed some space to grow. (*Washington Post*, March 30, 2000, p. 20)

Without mentioning the activists or their illegal broadcasting, this piece sided with the regulators of the airwaves and used an organic metaphor of "growth" to support the new LPFM licensing scheme.

The *New York Times* made only passing mention to micro radio on their editorial page. In an editorial titled, "Last Minute Congressional Mischief," it drew attention to a number of significant bills that were being attached as riders to larger appropriations bills. Though Clinton had vowed to veto the anti-LPFM legislation as a stand-alone bill, members of Congress knew his choices were more limited if the legislation was included as a rider. The *Times* described the radio preservation act as, "a rider pushed by commercial broadcasters that would hinder the FCC from approving low-power radio licenses for groups like schools and churches that want to reach communities underserved by commercial radio" (*New York Times*, October 19, 2000, p. A32).

This relatively neutral wording contrasted with a *Washington Post* editorial that addressed the same issue. The *Post* did not buy the industry's argument about interference. "The claim is that low-power stations would cause interference. The reality, at least for most opponents, is fear of competition" (*Washington Post*, October 27, 2000, p. A34). It drew attention to a theme repeated by activists and later picked up by Kennard: the idea that interference was a smokescreen for market protection. It went on to encourage President Clinton to support LPFM in spite of congressional maneuvers to force his hand. "He should ensure that in any final deal the commission has the authority to go forward with its program" (*Washington Post,* October 27, 2000, p. A34).

Picking up the theme of the NAB acting to protect market share as it sought to kill LPFM, the *St. Petersburg Times* published a scathing editorial on the eve of passage of the radio preservation act.

Give them credit for their candor, The Radio Preservation Act does just that—preserves the dominance of commercial broadcasters to profit from the airwaves in the FM dial. Industry supporters in Congress know what they're doing; the legislation would keep small, community stations off the dial, concentrate licensing power in Congress' hands and keep campaign cash flowin. (*St. Petersburg Times,* December 22, 2000, p. A22)

This editorial attempted to lift the rhetorical veil of "interference" replacing it with, "follow the money." The discourse of broadcast policy as determined by moneyed interests was invoked, eliminating the FCC from the process and charging commercial broadcasters with the wholesale purchase of Congress. The editorial accused the broadcast industry of "using the deceit that low-power radio interferes with existing stations" (*St. Petersburg Times,* December 22, 2000, p. A22). This piece also drew attention to the process of dis-empowering the FCC: "The legislation also shifts authority on low-power licenses from the FCC to Congress, thereby ensuring the broadcast industry will use campaign donations to keep its interests the priority of Congress" (*St. Petersburg Times,* December 22, 2000, p. A22). The discourse of corporate control of government could not be any stronger. This newspaper was boldly critiquing corporate influence on broadcast policy and placing this in the context of campaign finance issues.

Finally, on Christmas day 2000, the *Washington Post* printed an editorial connecting the issues of interference and market protection. Though broadcasters had consistently trumpeted the issue of spectrum interference as their sole objection to LPFM, this editorial stated otherwise.

The broadcasters emerged victorious last week, as Congress passes—as part of the budget deal—a provision radically scaling back the low-power initiative. And it is worth noting that the language orders the FCC not merely to study the potential for interference but also to examine "the economic impact" on "incumbent FM radio broadcasters." Turns out market protection was an issue after all. (*Washington Post,* December 25, 2000, p. A44)

Though the NAB had never publicly argued for further research into the economic impact of LPFM, the congressional bill supported by the NAB added this concept to a debate that had been taking place for more than two years. With this provision one might view the term "interference" with new associations. The NAB's opposition may not have been founded out of concern for the unfortunate radio listener who experienced static on their clock radio—because of an errant micro station broadcasting the latest thoughts of Mumia Abu Jamal—as they desperately try to tune in the satellite feed of classic rock. No, the *Post* was arguing that the NAB feared the loss of audience and in turn advertising revenue, because a diverse market is a fragmented niche market much like cable television, where special interests (golf, cooking, music etc.) now have their own channel.

The passage of the bill is a sad triumph of powerful campaign donors over reasonable policy. Whatever legitimate interference questions remained—and some probably did—the answer should not have been rescinding the commission's licensing authority or making that power contingent on a subsequent act of Congress. Given the power of the broadcasters on Capital Hill, they now effectively will have a veto over any effort to permit more liberal licensing once the FCC conducts the required studies. We have a hunch that whatever those studies show about interference, that veto will be used. (*Washington Post,* December 25, 2000, p. A44)

Thus the knowledge and practice of small scale, illegal broadcasting moved from "pirate" status to "reasonable policy" in the eyes of one of the nation's most prominent newspapers. And with the passage of the radio preservation act, another connection was made linking the power of money and politics. Though the micro radio community might be sympathetic to the ideas of campaign finance reform, this was not a significant piece of their discourse. Nevertheless, the events that unfolded as a result of the movement's activities prompted the editorial boards of a few major newspapers to connect broadcast policy and corporate influence on the political system.

   The bashing of big business while supporting the little guy has been an enduring news value for a long time (Gans, 1979). The newspaper support of the micro radio cause may well have had as much to do with newsroom practices and familiar story patterns than with any deep commitment to micro radio.

The virtue of smallness comes through most clearly in stories that deal with the faults of bigness, for in the news, Big Government, Big labor, and Big Business, rarely have virtues. Bigness is feared, among other things, as impersonal and inhuman. . . . As such bigness is a threat to individualism and an enduring value in the news. (Gans, 1979, p. 49)

Thus, reporters could easily cast the story in the familiar metaphor of David and Goliath, the micro broadcasters against the global media giants. And because the technology being advocated was old technology, outlawed twenty years ago, there was no fear of the "dangers" of micro radio as something new and terrifying. As an older, smaller technology, micro radio represented a connection to the past and brought with it all the nostalgia of a small town, community broadcasting that never existed in the past. Micro radio may have served as a "surrogate" for the past, for "tradition." (Gans, 1979). Though activists may have had a radically different vision of the potential of micro radio, the enduring news values of "small is good" and "the past is good" may have aided the movement as reporters reached for familiar ways to tell this new story of media activism.

   In contrast to a well documented tension between dominant media and social movements (Gitlin, 1980; Olien, Tichnor, & Donohue, 1989), in this instance the dominant national press provided extensive positive coverage of the micro radio struggle. Beyond the issue of news values, this support news coverage can be traced in part to the organization and participation of the diverse range of movement participants. From the grassroots broadcasters who put new content on the air to the policy and academic researchers who put the anecdotal ideas and practices into a lager context, this emerging movement harnessed the collective skills of a host of participants to create an truly effective campaign for social change. Despite the history of media's attempts to mute or limit the voices of social change, this campaign garnered widespread support and demonstrated the power and potential of a well organized media reform movement.

CONCLUSION

The print media was kind to the micro radio movement and provided a large public platform for the presentation of the movement's ideas. From profiles of local broadcasters to emphatic editorials, the major newspapers played a significant role in advancing the micro radio discourse. If a movement's success is measured by the degree to which its ideas are disseminated and integrated into established social institutions and discourses, the representations examined here suggest a movement that was rather effective at molding the cognitive terrain of micro radio into a socially acceptable form. The extended defense of micro radio by Chairman Kennard is a testament to the power of the discourse of public media access and diversity. Though the specific micro radio policy has been stymied for the moment, the structure of the media activism and reform movement appears to have been strengthened by engaging the micro radio struggle.

Returning to the comparison with the environmental movement, the spotted owl controversy was not *solved* by the designation of the owl as an endangered species. Logging practices continue that threaten the bird's survival and pressures to ease restrictions on logging never cease. Nevertheless, the environmental movement, particularly in the Pacific Northwest, was strengthened through the work to defend this bird. Networks were established, discursive terrain mapped and articulated, alliances formed and oppositions identified. The same can be said of micro radio. Media consolidation and the struggle to allow local communities to access media technology in noncommercial ways will be an ongoing struggle for some time. What this chapter revealed is that the dominant media (in this case print media) can play a significant role in distributing a social movement's discourse. The representation of a movement discourse can be problematic and subject to misrepresentation or marginalization. Fortunately for the micro radio community, the dominant press gave the activists fair space to make their case and in many instances, came to the aid of the cause through overt editorial support.

5

Micro Radio and the Government: Looking for Activist Discourse in FCC Policy

In January 2000, the FCC issued a "Report and Order" (No. 99-25) that established the process of licensing LPFM. This document was a significant piece of the government's attempt to license micro radio. This chapter looks closely at this document. The FCC "Report and Order" is examined for evidence of the social struggle over LPFM. Were the key players represented in this document? Were the micro radio activists represented and if so, who was cited and how was their position related to the document? What were the major issues within the "Report and Order" and how were the key players positioned around these issues? These are the question that will guide the reading of this policy document as we continue to trace the movement of the micro radio discourse from the internal world of the activists, through the media and finally into government policy itself.

As stated previously, this study is grounded on the social movement model described by Eyerman and Jamison (1991). This cognitive model asserts that social movements are a site of knowledge production. A historically specific juncture is needed for the knowledge produced by a social movement to gain widespread exposure. In this case, the issue of micro radio allowed significant pieces of the knowledge produced by the media activism and reform movement to coalesce. Micro radio became the site where the activists could publicly demonstrate the cognitive terrain established by the movement. This terrain included such concepts as public access to media technology, the reinvigoration of the public interest standard, the importance of localism, the value of independent media production, the need for diversity of media content and production, and a host of other issues about the connections between media and a pluralistic, democratic society. Just as the environmental movement needed a specific issue such as protecting the whales to demonstrate the value of species protection, the media activism and reform movement needed (and continues to need) specific issues to demonstrate the importance of public access to media technology.

As demonstrated in the previous chapters, activists used the Internet as a coordinating tool to work though the specific ideas and practices of the movement. Part of the terrain explored and defined by a movement includes practices. Eyerman and Jamison (1991) define this as cognitive praxis. In the case of micro radio, the technical information about how to build and maintain a micro radio station was part of the cognitive praxis that was developed. As the movement progressed, the specific legal skills needed to mount challenges to FCC enforcement became another realm of cognitive praxis, as did the specific details of how to apply to the FCC, how to gain local support for LPFM, how to build coalitions, and how to lobby the national government. These skills and many others were developed and disseminated throughout the movement as the issue of micro radio moved from a fringe issue and onto the front page of the FCC web site.

Specific examples of activists working through issues on the MRN listserv have been examined and the representation of these activists' ideas and practices was examined through the dominant newspaper coverage. The newspaper coverage was one form of public display of the knowledge produced by this social movement. The policy realm was another significant area for the public display of movement knowledge. Just as the Endangered Species Act codified many of the central concepts of the environmental movement, the licensing of LPFM was a significant government policy document that codified some of the ideas contained within the media activism and reform movement.

FCC "REPORT AND ORDER," MM DOCKET NO. 99-25: THE CREATION OF LOW-POWER RADIO SERVICES

The FCC "Report and Order" creating LPFM service was an eighty-page document with detailed explanations for the shape and form of the final licensing scheme. Because of the detail provided in this document and the organizations cited to support the positions taken, this document provided an excellent opportunity for research into the connections between movement initiatives and public policy. The FCC received more than 3,000 comments regarding LPFM during the comment period and a handful of the individuals and organizations that submitted comments were cited in the final "Report and Order." The selection of these groups for inclusion in the final document was one measure of the strength of their arguments and their recognized role in helping to shape the emergence of a public policy. The FCC position on a range of issues is examined in the context of the groups and individuals cited who either supported or opposed the final FCC decision.

The FCC "Report and Order" creating LPFM addressed many of the issues raised throughout the debate about micro radio. The FCC addressed all concerns about ownership, localism and commercial influence in the final ruling. The following section will focus on the FCC's resolution of questions about the following issues: (a) public interest obligations, (b) commercial vs. noncommercial designation, (c) ownership restrictions, (d) amnesty for pirates, and (e) technical issues.

The FCC organized the "Report and Order" around these issues specifically as they were the areas that generated the most controversy among those who submitted comments.

THE PUBLIC INTEREST AND LPFM

The concept of the public interest is present throughout the FCC "Report and Order." As this research has shown, the activists were divided as to whether this was an effective concept to employ in the struggle over micro radio. Some activists viewed public interest standards as a powerful regulatory tool to hold broadcasters accountable while others saw it as a political concept that was used to limit the range of voices on radio or television. Despite the activists concerns about this concept, the FCC repeatedly invoked the public interest as a central component of the rationale for LPFM. In the introduction to the "Report and Order," the FCC wrote:

We believe that the LPFM service authorized in this proceeding will provide opportunities for new voices to be heard and will ensure that we fulfill our statutory obligation to authorize facilities in a manner that best serves the public interest. (FCC Report and Order 99-25, 2000, p. 2)

Throughout the report, the FCC equated LPFM with the public interest, invoking a connection between small-scale local media and service to community needs. Citing their "statutory obligation," the FCC put their decision in the context of broadcast policy history, possibly in anticipation of the attacks that would be mounted against this policy.

The FCC noted the large number of comments from diverse groups they received in response to the "Notice of Proposed Rulemaking" (FCC, 1999) and cited the widespread public desire for LPFM as an indication of the importance of the new micro radio policy.

These comments—from churches or other religious organizations, students, labor unions, community organizations and activists, musicians, and other citizens—reflect a broad interest in service from highly local radio stations strongly grounded in their communities. In authorizing this new service today, we enhance locally focused community-oriented radio broadcasting. (FCC, 2000, p. 3)

The media activism and reform movement can be seen in the list of organizations who submitted comments supporting LPFM. The FCC's proclamation that the new rule would "enhance locally focused community-oriented radio broadcasting" was an indication of the acceptance of the movement's discourse, where the regulatory agency picked up and supported the idea that a broad-based constituency would benefit from expanded community media.

One area where the activists and the commercial broadcasters were in agreement was in response to the FCC plan to license 1,000-watt micro stations. These stations would cover an area far greater than the proposed 10- and 100-watt designations. The micro radio activists opposed the 1,000-watt class because they feared that one large station could dominate a region and limit the number of smaller stations that might be able to coexist in a given area. The commercial broadcasters opposed the 1,000-watt class of station out of "interference" concerns, though the competition issue lay just below the surface. The FCC noted:

Generally speaking, the proposal to authorize LP1000 stations generated the most controversy among the commenters. The topic was one of the few areas that generated opposition by both current full service broadcasters and low power radio proponents, although for different reasons. (FCC, 2000, p. 5)

The combined opposition to the larger stations resulted in the FCC's decision to drop the 1,000 watt class of service.

The record, including comments from both current broadcasters and public interest groups who were opposed to stations as large as 1000 watts, convinces us that licensing such a service is not in the public interest. (FCC, 2000, p. 7)

Thus the larger stations were dropped in part because they were not seen to serve the public interest. This raised interesting questions about the current broadcast regulatory scheme where large, centrally owned and operated stations dominate the radio dial. One cannot but wonder why large micro stations do not serve the public interest while large commercial stations do. One obvious answer is that the public interest groups were aligned with the commercial broadcasters in this case, whereas public interest opposition to media expansion and consolidation often contradicts the position of commercial broadcasters.

The connection between micro radio and the public interest was articulated by the FCC in the Programming and Service Rules section of the report. This section dealt with whether the public interest obligations that apply to full power commercial broadcasters should apply to micro stations. The FCC found that fewer obligations would be necessary for micro stations because of the very nature of the technology.

Every broadcast licensee is required to operate its station in the public interest. Given the nature of the LPFM service, however, we conclude that certain obligations imposed on full-power radio licensees would be unnecessary if applied to LPFM licensees. We expect that the local nature of this service, coupled with the eligibility and selection criteria we are adopting, will ensure that LPFM licensees will meet the needs and interests of their communities. (FCC, 2000, p. 66)

There is a certain irony here. The micro radio activists had argued that the commercial broadcasters had effectively eliminated their public interest service and this had in part created the need for micro radio to replace this service. On the other hand, the NAB argued that all stations should be treated equally and public interest standards should be applied to all broadcasters regardless of size. This raises the question of whether the public interest has any appreciable power as a regulatory concept? If commercial broadcasters were meeting their public interest obligations, then why would micro radio be necessary? And if micro radio was intended to expand public interest broadcasting, why are the public interest obligations lower and not more rigorous for micro broadcasters? These questions reveal the ambiguous nature of the public interest standard and the lack of uniform application of this standard across broadcast formats. This conclusion supports Streeter's (1996) argument that concepts such as the public interest serve primarily to reinforce a liberal regulatory scheme that serves the interests of commercial media at the expense of a diverse public.

COMMERCIAL VERSUS NONCOMMERCIAL LPFM

As the debate within the micro radio community revealed, the issue of commercial versus noncommercial radio posed a set of complex questions. The FCC asked for public comments regarding this issue in their "Notice of Proposed Rulemaking" (FCC, 1999). In summarizing the comments addressing commercialism, the FCC wrote, "Of those commenters supporting LPFM, an overwhelming majority endorsed establishing it as a noncommercial service" (FCC, 2000, p. 8). The FCC followed the will of the majority of comment submissions and designated LPFM to be noncommercial. The FCC noted many of the themes raised by the activists in explaining their rationale for the noncommercial designation. Specifically, the FCC acknowledged the potential negative influences of audience maximization and profit incentive when attempting to serve niche populations and interest groups. Thus the FCC established the new micro stations under the designation, NCE: noncommercial educational.

Commercial broadcast stations, by their very nature, have commercial incentives to maximize audience size in order to improve their ratings and thereby increase their advertising revenues. We are concerned that these commercial incentives could frustrate achievement of our goal in establishing this service: to foster a program service responsive to the needs and interests of small local community groups, particularly specialized community needs that have not been well served by commercial broadcast stations. We believe that noncommercial licensees, which are not subject to commercial imperatives to maximize audience size, are more likely than commercial licensees to serve small, local groups with particular shared needs and interests, such as linguistic and cultural minorities or groups with shared civic or educational interests that may now be underserved by advertiser-supported commercial radio and higher powered noncommercial radio stations. (FCC, 2000, p. 9)

In this case, the idea that a large audience equaled public service was inverted. The NAB consistently argued that the best measure of their public service was the size of their audience. If no one was listening, no one was being served. This was the classic market model of the public interest where the public was conceived of as an audience and service was measured in ratings. The argument put forth by the FCC in establishing noncommercial LPFM was predicated on a freedom from demands to maximize audience and deliver specific audience demographics to advertisers. The narrow focus of LPFM content was intended to reach specific communities and not necessarily appeal to broad audiences. This model contradicted the primary broadcast regulatory scheme and ran counter to the "market" model of neo-liberalism. The model the FCC chose for LPFM was closer to a public sphere model of public service, where the public was conceived as diverse citizens in need of information with which to better participate in and enrich society. By choosing to base LPFM on a public sphere model, the question arises; if niche programming is valued and worthwhile at the smallest level of radio, why is it not emphasized in the regulations of larger commercial and noncommercial stations?

Another issue that was raised by activists, though was not addressed by the FCC, was the question of how small community groups would be expected to fund their stations given a noncommercial designation? The FCC acknowledged the issue though offered no remedy.

While we have considered the entrepreneurial opportunities that low power radio stations might create, we nonetheless conclude that a noncommercial service would best serve the Commission's goals of bringing additional diversity to radio broadcasting and serving local community needs in a focused manner. (FCC, 2000, p. 9)

The effect of excluding *any* commercial version of LPFM meant that only non-profit organizations with significant resources would be able to build, maintain and staff micro stations. The FCC noted that by establishing LPFM as noncommercial, a debate about the impact of LPFM on the economics of radio broadcasting would be avoided (FCC, 2000). At the same time, this arrangement created a high hurdle for small stations to get up and running without the option of advertising revenue. This solution can be seen as a direct response to the established broadcast industry where LPFM stations potential to compete (for both limited advertising dollars and audience share) was severely hobbled by the entirely noncommercial designation.

Finally, the FCC addressed the issue of "educational" classification in the NCE designation. The NCE category was said to be broad enough to encompass a range of issues, many of which would qualify as "educational" programming.

We have also stated that "in order to qualify as an educational station, it is not necessary that the proposed programming be exclusively educational." Given the latitude that entities have under our rules to qualify as NCEs, we do not believe that limiting eligibility for LPFM licenses to NCEs will unduly limit the range of groups that will be eligible to apply for LPFM licenses or the services that they can provide. (FCC, 2000, pp. 10–11)

This somewhat contradictory position stated that the NCE classification would increase diversity and community service at the same time that the designation was not specific enough to present significant barriers to participation. The "latitude" in the NCE designation may have allowed for a variety of organizations to obtain licenses. At the same time it was the regulatory latitude within the NCE classification that had allowed the larger, established NCE broadcasters (most NPR stations among others) to adopt their current formats. The activists charged many of the established NCE stations with abandoning their local communities and resorting to homogenized, satellite fed programming. The question raised by the FCC decision to designate LPFM as NCE was: what will prevent the low power service from replicating the alleged shortcomings of traditional NCE stations? The FCC appeared to believe that the small-scale nature of the broadcasting would inherently manifest local programming.

OWNERSHIP RESTRICTIONS

One of the issues that recurred throughout the activists' listserv debate was the issue of micro station ownership. From the activists' perspective, any plan to license LPFM would have to include restrictions that would prevent the micro stations from being consolidated under a handful of the commercial media conglomerates. LPFM regulations would then have to run counter to the regulatory trend of relaxed ownership restrictions that has reconfigured the media landscape in the wake of the 1996 Telecommunications Act. In their "Notice of Proposed Rulemaking" (FCC, 1999), the FCC acknowledged this ownership issue and requested comments on the question of who should be allowed to own the new micro stations. Summarizing their request, the FCC wrote:

We proposed to prohibit any person or entity with an attributable interest in a broadcast station from having an ownership interest in any LPFM station in any market. We sought comment on whether the proposed strict cross-ownership restrictions would unnecessarily prevent individuals and entities with valuable broadcast experience from contributing to the success of the LPFM service. We also asked for comment on whether broadcasters with an attributable interest in broadcasting stations should be allowed to establish an LPFM station in a community where they do not have an attributable broadcast interest. (FCC, 2000, p. 12)

In this request for comments, the FCC questioned the value of media concentration, though the question was applied to a class of service that had yet to be established. The same questions could be posed to established broadcasters. The FCC determined LPFM to be unique and therefore subject to variations from traditional regulation.

The presence of the ownership issue in this series of FCC documents pointed to a measure of effectiveness on the part of the media activism and reform movement. The effects of concentration of ownership were a central concern of this movement, a concern that had slowly been recognized by a wider segment of society (newspapers, local, state and federal government officials, etc.) as a significant influence on the democratic process. While the dominant media were consolidating at an unprecedented rate, the FCC was preparing a new radio service that would respond to that consolidation with rules diametrically opposed to dominant regulatory policy. Predictably, the NAB responded to the FCC question about ownership rules by opposing any restrictions.

The NAB opposes restricting current broadcasters from low power ownership, claiming that consolidation of ownership in fact increases diversity of broadcast formats because of economic efficiencies. The NAB further alleges that such a prohibition would preclude low power stations from realizing efficiencies through joint operations with a full power counterpart. (FCC, 2000, p. 12)

The NAB argued that consolidation "increases diversity." This statement was an indication of the gulf of understanding between the activists and the commercial broadcasters. Either the NAB was being wholly disingenuous or they were attempting to spin an issue to their favor. Either way, the issue of whether existing broadcasters should be allowed to own LPFM stations elicited vastly different reactions from the key players in this debate. The FCC noted the activists' position in their citation of the comments of the National Lawyers Guild and the United Church of Christ (UCC).

The National Lawyers Guild, for example, asks why the Commission would allow the few companies who already hold a broadcast license also to hold a low power license when 99.9 percent of the American people are barred from using the most effective communications media in the nation. . . . UCC, et al., adds that not only should such agreements between full power licensees and low power licensees be prohibited, but also that agreements of a similar nature between two or more low power licensees should be disallowed. (FCC, 2000, p. 13)

Again the FCC quoted the discourse propagated by participants of the media activism and reform movement. The movement discourse moved from listserv discussions and policy statements from individuals and institutions, into the pages of national government regulatory policy. Given the final FCC decision on this issue, the presence of the activists' discourse in this document can be seen as providing persuasive ground which the FCC could use to support the new policy. One can only speculate on whether the FCC would rule similarly in the absence of the activist discourse. The connection between the activist discourse and the final FCC decision is one indication that the activist discourse prevailed and that individuals within the FCC found merit in the arguments put forth in support of LPFM.

In their decision on the issue of ownership restrictions, the FCC made a strong case for limitations and linked their case to the larger issue of media diversity:

We conclude that our interest in providing for new voices to speak to the community, and providing a medium for new speakers to gain experience in the field, would be best served by barring cross-ownership between LPFM licensees and existing broadcast owners and other media entities. This prohibition is national and absolute in nature, unlike our existing cross-media ownership rules. Thus, for example, a newspaper cannot have an attributable interest in any LPFM station, regardless of whether the newspaper and LPFM station are co-located. We believe our interest in promoting diversity warrants such a strict approach. (FCC, 2000, pp. 12–13)

Here again, the FCC made a special case for LPFM, contradicting the regulatory policies that determined the other established media. One reading of this would be that LPFM was so small and ineffective as to not warrant the same policies that shape larger stations. Another perspective might be that LPFM was so effective and important to localism that special regulations are warranted. Either way, the dominant regulatory scheme was brought into question. If LPFM was small and irrelevant, why not allow traditional ownership rules to apply? On the other hand, if LPFM was an effective tool for promoting localism and diversity, why not amend the rules that regulate larger stations to match the rules of LPFM, thus promoting localism and diversity across the entire radio dial? Clearly, the later concept would be politically untenable given the power and influence of the NAB. Nevertheless, the FCC's decision to support the activist position on LPFM ownership marked the successful deployment of discursive strategies on the part of the activists at the same time that it provided a crack in the dominant regulatory scheme.

A second component of the ownership restrictions addressed the issue of whether LPFM applicants should be community based. Although the NCE designation had been decided, the FCC still had to resolve how to define whether an organization was "community based" and if that included a residency requirement. Noting that most commenters supported a locally based requirement (FCC, 2000, p. 14), the FCC outlined the details of how this requirement would be implemented.

This service is intended to respond to the highly local interests that are not necessarily being met by full-power stations. Furthermore, since LPFM will be a noncommercial educational service, we cannot rely on commercial market forces and business incentives to ensure that local needs are fulfilled. Given the small coverage of LPFM stations, and our intention that the particular needs and interests of these small areas be served, local familiarity is more significant than it might be for a station serving a larger area and population. (FCC, 2000, p. 15)

The FCC set up a distinction between the type of programming determined by market forces and the programming developed by NCE stations. Again this affirmed the contentions of the activists while it contrasts with dominant broadcast policy. Attempting to define local residency, the FCC came up with a fairly restrictive formula:

All LPFM applicants must be based within 10 miles of the station they seek to operate. This means that the applicant must be able to certify that it or its local chapter or branch is physically headquartered, has a campus, or has 75 percent of its board members residing within 10 miles of the reference coordinates of the proposed transmitting antenna. We chose the 10-mile distance as proportionate to most stations' likely effective reach. (FCC, 2000, p. 15)

This residency requirement was another way the FCC sought to limit the ability of national organizations to hijack a service designed to allow local people to speak to one another.

The final issue regarding ownership restrictions dealt with national and local ownership limits. Initially, the FCC sought comments on a five- or ten-station national ownership cap. The FCC noted that civil rights organizations and the United Church of Christ all favored a one-station-per-owner limit (FCC, 2000, p. 17). However, the NAB "does not believe that a national ownership cap is allowed under the 1996 act, and believes that common ownership will improve efficiency in the service" (FCC, 2000, p. 17). The FCC again sided with the activist perspective, allowing only one station per owner on a national basis. A two-year waiting period was established as LPFM service came into being. After that waiting period, if available frequencies were unfilled, organizations would be eligible to own up to five stations. Three years later, the national cap would be raised to 10 stations

(FCC, 2000, p.18). Thus, organizations with greater resources would be able to broadcast on unused frequencies.

In response to the NAB allegation that ownership caps would be in violation of the 1996 Act, the FCC wrote:

Section 202 of the Telecommunications Act of 1996 (the 1996 Act) eliminating national multiple ownership restrictions for existing full power commercial stations does not apply to a new broadcast service. Given our decision to limit LPFM to noncommercial educational broadcasters, Section 202 clearly does not apply to LPFM and we need not discuss this issue further. (FCC, 2000, p. 18)

Thus, the FCC reaffirmed their authority to regulate the airwaves and essentially told the NAB to stop raising this issue. By choosing to designate LPFM as noncommercial educational broadcasters, they made a clear choice to circumvent the ownership laws of the 1996 Act. The NCE designation allowed the FCC to institute the most restrictive ownership caps in recent history, reversing a regulatory trend begun in the 1980s. This was yet another instance where the LPFM policy contained regulations that contrasted with dominant regulatory policy.

The FCC followed a similar course in regard to local ownership issues, despite opposition to any restrictions from the NAB. "The NAB opposes the proposed ban on common ownership, saying that common ownership leads to increased efficiencies" (FCC, 2000, p. 19). From the comments cited by the FCC, it appeared that "efficiency" was the dominant discourse deployed by the NAB in response to any regulation of LPFM. The consistent rejection of the efficiency argument by the FCC signaled the weakness of the NAB's ability to establish an effective discourse to promote their agenda. Again, the National Lawyers Guild and Civil Rights Organizations were cited as representatives of the many groups supporting a limit of one station per owner per community. The FCC sided with the activists and established a local ownership limit of one station per owner per community.

We will restrict local ownership and allow one entity to own only one LPFM station in a "community." We concur with those commenters who expressed concern over the potential for diminution of diversity in ownership if one entity were allowed to control more than one station in their community. (FCC, 2000, p. 19)

The local ownership restrictions matched the national rules with the stated goal of fostering diversity. This series of ownership restrictions matched the primary goals of most of the micro radio activists. The sympathetic response of the FCC to the issues of ownership and diversity can be seen as a measure of success on the part of the movement to both move their discourse into a dominant political policy institution (FCC) and codify the discourse in public policy. That the NAB position was consistently rejected despite the history of the political influence of the commercial broadcast lobby reflected the weakness of the NAB's discourse and the strength of the political will of individuals such as FCC Chairman William Kennard. In confronting and contradicting the wishes of the NAB, Kennard stood in defense of his vision of the public interest while creating a political firestorm that would eventually spread beyond the FCC and into the halls of Congress.

AMNESTY FOR PIRATES

One of the concerns of the activists that recurred throughout the listserv discussion and appeared in the newspaper coverage as well was the question of whether the people who advanced the issue of micro radio would be allowed to benefit from the FCC licensing scheme. The activists likened themselves to Rosa Parks, invoking a tradition of civil disobedience to confront unjust laws. Micro broadcasters who went on the air illegally to protest the FCC ban on low power radio hoped that the FCC would acknowledge the value of their efforts and not penalize them by banning them from eligibility to possess an LPFM license. For all broadcast license applicants, the FCC used a set of "character qualifications" that incorporated exclusions for criminal convictions, including illegal broadcasting. Activists hoped the FCC would make an exception for LPFM protestors convicted of illegal broadcasting and allow them to apply for the new licenses.

In their "Notice of Proposed Rulemaking" (FCC, 1999), the FCC sought comment on a compromise position where applications would be accepted:

from parties who have broadcast illegally, but who either (1) promptly ceased operation when advised by the commission to do so, or (2) voluntarily ceased operation within ten days of the publication of the *Notice* in the *Federal Register*. (FCC, 2000, p. 21)

The response to this proposal fell along predictable lines. The activist community was divided over supporting the compromise or pushing for complete amnesty while the broadcast industry rejected the compromise and pointed out the irony of allowing "pirates" to own stations while excluding existing broadcasters.

The National Lawyers Guild and the Civil Rights Organizations both argue for amnesty for unlicensed broadcasters. Many individuals insist that without radio "pirates," LPFM would not have been created. Others, such as Amherst and UCC, et al., support the middle ground set forth in the *Notice*, saying that it is most fair to the interests of future low power broadcasters and to the public. The Alliance for Community Media also supports the Commission's proposed compromise. Many commenters believe that anyone who has operated illegally should not be eligible for a license. NAB believes that because "pirate" broadcasters operated illegally, they should not be excused or granted amnesty. Some object to restricting parties with an interest in a broadcast station from owning an LPFM station, but allowing "pirates" to own them. (FCC, 2000, p. 21)

The FCC responded to this range of comments by adopting their original compromise proposal. Thus activists were denied a blanket amnesty, though micro broadcasters who responded to FCC enforcement by shutting down retained their license eligibility. Given the position of the NAB and the fact that many micro broadcasters continued to broadcast illegally after the FCC notice, the decision to compromise on the character qualifications issue did not fully meet the goals of either the supporters or opponents of LPFM. With neither side satisfied, this issue remained a point of contention and became a focus of the NAB as they moved the issue into the U.S. Congress.

TECHNICAL ISSUES

The primary argument used by the NAB in its opposition to LPFM was based around the issue of radio interference. The NAB contended that the radio dial (spectrum) was significantly congested as it was and that the addition of numerous small stations would result in widespread interference for all radio listeners. This accusation resulted in a number of technical studies that attempted to resolve the question of low power interference. These studies and the FCC's attempt to balance the competing information form the basis of the technical standards the FCC adopted in the their LPFM rulemaking. Although the FCC addressed questions about possible low power AM broadcasting or if television channel 6 broadcast frequencies (82–88 MHz, frequencies adjacent to designated FM frequencies 87.9–108 MHz) should be assigned to low-power FM, the biggest area of dispute was over the separation between radio stations (FCC, 2000). The spacing of stations on the radio dial was termed, "second and third adjacent channel protection" (FCC, 2000, p. 31).

What this terminology refers to is how closely stations may be placed on the radio dial in a given area. Prior to the LPFM initiative, FCC policy dictated that no two stations could occupy that same frequency or the frequency on either side (first adjacent). This means that a station broadcasting at 90.1 MHz would be protected from a station broadcasting at 89.9 MHz and 90.3 MHz. Furthermore, most stations were given second adjacent channel protection effectively adding 89.7 MHz and 90.5 MHz to the list of protected frequencies in the previous example. Third adjacent channel protection expands the protected frequencies one step further and was the dominant standard for station spacing. The FCC dropped third adjacent channel protection "for certain grandfathered and short spaced stations in 1997" and there were close to 300 full-power stations operating without third adjacent protection in 2000 (FCC, 2000, p. 31).

In describing the background to the channel protection issue, the FCC noted exceptions to the third adjacency standard and sought comment on a proposal to allow LPFM stations to be placed within a standard of second adjacent channel protection. In making this proposal, the FCC noted the existence of stations operating with this standard.

With regard to 2nd-adjacent channel protection, we noted that "grandfathered" short-spaced FM facilities were permitted to modify their facilities without regard to 2nd- and 3rd-adjacent channel spacings during the period from 1964 to 1987, and from 1997 to the present. We indicated that no interference complaints were received as a result of those modifications and found that the small risk of interference was outweighed by improved service. Similarly, we noted that we have been willing in the past to accept small amounts of potential 2nd- and 3rd-adjacent channel interference in the noncommercial FM service where such interference is counterbalanced by substantial service gains. (FCC, 2000, p. 31)

The proposal to alter spacing standards and allow LPFM stations to potentially interfere with commercial broadcasters inspired technical studies sponsored by the (1) NAB, (2) the Consumer's Electronic Manufacturers Association (CEMA) in cooperation with NPR, (3) the National Lawyers Guild, and (4) the FCC Office of Engineering and Technology (OET). A fifth study by broadcast engineer Theodore Rappaport on behalf of the Media Access Project was a review of the other four studies. The findings of these studies reflected possible variations within the scientific method and the discrepancies between these studies formed the basis for the dispute about adjacent channel protection.

The technical issues involved in these studies are outside the scope of this research. It is significant that the competing interest groups stuggled over the language used to describe the research and the way concepts, such as "interference."

The NAB study was said to be based on twenty-eight different FM radios using the highest standard (50 dB signal-to-noise ratio) of interference protection of any of the studies. (When measuring signal to noise ratio, a higher dB value indicates a lower, more desirable signal to noise ratio.) Accordingly, the NAB study found the most "interference" because they used a higher standard to define interference.

Based on its performance measure, NAB indicates that 15 to 22 of the 28 receivers in its sample would experience interference from signals on 3rd-adjacent channels at the current −40 dB D/U protection ratio. NAB also indicates that 22 to 23 receivers in its sample would experience interference from signals on 2nd-adjacent channels. NAB therefore concludes that FM receivers generally do not perform up to the current FCC interference standards and that the Commission's assumptions that these restrictions could be eliminated for LPFM stations are incorrect. (FCC, 2000, p. 33)

The NAB attempted to demonstrate that interference already existed on the FM dial and that current radios were not meeting FCC standards for interference. Given this, any additional stations were out of the question according to the NAB. CEMA's study established 45 dB as a target for audio quality (contrasted with the FCC standard of 20 dB) and tested sixteen consumer radios for interference from broadcasters operating at various separations of channel protection. CEMA found that only stations operating with third adjacent protection met their interference goal and thus maintained that third adjacent channel protection should be maintained.

The FCC responded to the NAB and CEMA by questioning their use of higher interference standards than are currently employed by the FCC:

Both CEMA and NAB used an audio signal-to-noise criterion to define acceptable FM service. CEMA used a S/N value of 45 dB based on an earlier study by NPR. NAB chose a 50 dB S/N criteria. . . . We do not find the audio S/N criteria suggested by either CEMA or NAB to be appropriate interference criteria for today's FM radio service. . . . While NAB and CEMA may desire that FM radio service be protected to higher levels of service, based on NAB's earlier study and the results of the technical studies before us herein, we do not believe that the existing interference protection standards, e.g., the 20 dB co-channel interference requirement, generally provides for protection to such levels. . . . We therefore fail to see how 50 or 45 dB can be an appropriate measure when most radios do not perform at this level, even in the absence of any interference as was the case in NAB's tests. We have no reason to find that the vast majority of current FM receivers do not provide satisfactory service to the public and therefore believe that a lower value or measure of acceptable performance would be more appropriate for interference purposes. (FCC, 2000, p. 34)

Thus the FCC largely rejected the NAB and CEMA studies. The NAB attempted to make the case that more protection against is needed because they found interference when they used a finer measurement. The FCC responded that if the current broadcast situation was as bad as the NAB study demonstrated, the public would be complaining and the FCC had no significant evidence of widespread public dissatisfaction with current levels of interference.

Taking a position that was almost the mirror image of the NAB position, the National Lawyers Guild (NLG) study raised the question of the definition of interference given the ability to detect electronic distortion beyond the range of human perception.

NLG indicated that it was difficult to establish a definition of unacceptable interference, noting that its tests demonstrated that even the best receivers showed measurable, often imperceptible, increases in distortion in the presence of extremely low level undesired signals . . . actual FM listening conditions are dependent on such variables as reception conditions, baseline radio performance without interference, and the various sounds and effects that interference can create. NLG stated that these variables make it difficult to scientifically derive a universal measure of unacceptable interference. (FCC, 2000, p. 34)

Thus the NLG study, instead of setting a numerical interference standard, questioned the ability to measure interference by one standard and noted the many complexities that create interference. The FCC's study done by their OET affirmed existing inference standards and pointed to the possibility of second adjacent placement of LPFM stations:

The OET study found that nearly all the receivers in the sample appear to meet or exceed the current 40 dB 2nd-adjacent channel protection requirement and to exceed the 3rd-adjacent channel protection by a wide margin. (FCC, 2000, p. 35)

The OET and NLG studies generally supported the FCC plan to occupy third adjacent channels although data about interference at the closer spacing second adjacent position spacing was inconclusive. The FCC summarized part of the two studies by when they wrote, "The OET and NLG studies generally conclude that FM receivers provide for adequate rejection of interference on 2nd- and 3rd-adjacent channels" (FCC, 2000, p. 40). Despite the limitations of these two studies, the FCC accepted the results and concluded that LPFM stations could be placed on both second and third adjacent channels without significant interference.

The Rappaport Study, funded by the Media Access Project was a meta analysis of the other studies and summarized the post-structural struggle to define interference. Ted Rappaport was the James S. Tucker Professor of Electrical Engineering at Virginia Tech and was one of thirty recipients of the 1992 National Science

Foundation Presidential Faculty Fellowship Awards. His analysis of the micro radio interference studies took aim at the industry-sponsored studies of the NAB and CEMA, pointing out their conceptual and methodological flaws. The FCC noted:

Rappaport asserts that there was a clear bias in some of the technical studies to overstate potential LPFM interference. He indicates, for example, that NAB omitted automobile radios (which make up over 20% of the radios sold and over 44% of the radios listened to by the public) from its LPFM impact study and made up a "worst-case" radio based on measurements from different radios.

Rappaport argues that in an academic setting, the design of NAB's and CEMA's tests would be considered flawed and the results from such tests would be disregarded. (FCC, 2000, p. 37)

Thus Rappaport, working for the Media Access Project, a significant institutional force in the LPFM struggle, invoked the rigor of academic research and discourse to discredit the industry-sponsored studies. This was another example of the way academic discourses can further a social movement, lending peer reviewed credibility through established, trusted research regimes.

The FCC decided to remove the third adjacent channel protections, although they did not go as far as removing the second adjacent protections. The FCC did not accept many of the findings of the NAB and CEMA studies. Instead they found the research and arguments submitted by their own engineers, the NLG and the Rappaport study to support reduced adjacency protection without significant increased interference:

We find that 100-watt LPFM stations operating on 3rd-adjacent channels will not result in significant new interference to the service of existing FM stations. Furthermore, we find that any small amount of interference that may occur in individual cases would be outweighed by the benefits of new low power FM service. With regard to 2nd-adjacent channel protection requirements, it appears that the risk of interference from LPFM signals on 2nd-adjacent channels may be somewhat higher. We find that this would also be true with regard to LPFM stations at power levels higher than 100 watts and antenna heights higher than 30 meters. Therefore, we will retain 2nd-adjacent channel protection requirements. (FCC, 2000, p. 42)

Thus the FCC attempted to balance the findings of five different studies. Each study was conducted by a key player in the micro radio debate and their theory, method and findings all bear the mark of their ideological perspective. Like the previous issues of ownership, commercialism, and so on, the NAB lost the discursive struggle over the particularities of the shape and form of LPFM. In each instance of policy formation, the activists were more heavily cited within the FCC report and their positions more closely affirmed in the final policy decision. Although we have seen that FCC Chairman William Kennard was a vocal advocate for LPFM by the time this policy document was drafted, the presence of the micro radio activists in the final document was a significant indication of the success the movement had in moving the cognitive terrain—localism, diversity and public access to the media—that was embodied in the micro radio issue from the virtual world of listserv and the ethers of the electromagnetic spectrum into the *Federal Register*. The LPFM *Rulemaking* marked a major success for the activists, having effectively convinced a traditionally industry friendly federal regulatory agency to adopt a set of rules vehemently opposed by established commercial *and* public broadcasters. Released in January 2000, this emblem of success from an emerging social movement about media and democracy would remain intact for less than a year however, as the broadcast industry turned to the U.S. Congress for relief.

6

U.S. Congress Intervenes: The Radio Broadcasting Perservation Act of 2000

Shortly after the FCC released their report in January 2000, legislation was introduced in the House of Representatives and the Senate to reverse the FCC decision. This legislation went through a number of congressional mutations, though never came up for a vote as a stand-alone bill. Instead, the bill was attached as a rider to the District of Columbia Appropriations Act, 2000 that was signed into law by President Clinton. Unlike the FCC report, the congressional legislation did not contain the detailed articulations of why particular decisions were made and what groups supported or opposed various provisions of the proposed law. From a historical perspective, this made tracing the discourse more difficult, as clear markers were not left in the written text. The process that led up to the passage of this legislation *was* documented through the transcript of a hearing of the House Commerce Committee as well as a floor debate in the House of Representatives. The following chapter examines the debate around congressional legislation known as the Radio Broadcasting Preservation Act of 2000 and summarizes the changes this legislation made to the FCC report. How Congress came to vote the way it did and the role of the activists in influencing that vote was examined through the historical documents found in the *Congressional Record*. The changes mandated by the Congress are self-evident, revealing intervention in a regulatory process that spanned two years, four engineering studies, and more than 3,000 public comments.

THE LEGISLATION

The congressional record on the Radio Broadcasting Preservation Act of 2000 shows that the struggle over low-power radio had moved from a tension between various members of the public and the government to a struggle between governmental agencies. By establishing a set of rules for LPFM, the FCC became the advocate for the new radio service to which Congress directed all its questions and criticisms. Although a limited group of representatives from the activist community as well as representatives from the commercial broadcasters took part in the February 17, 2000, FCC's Spectrum Management Responsibilities Hearing before the House Subcommittee on Telecommunications, Trade, and Consumer Protection of the Committee on Commerce, the bulk of the debate centered around the issue of whether the FCC had overstepped its authority and failed to consult Congress on this public policy issue. This intragovernmental struggle was documented in the transcripts of the House Commerce Committee hearing as well as a floor debate in the House. As we will see, the issue shifted from a policy debate about the value and virtues of community radio and became a struggle over who had the governmental authority to make such a policy change and what criteria would be used to justify the decision.

WHO MAKES THE RULES AROUND HERE?

From the outset of the Commerce Committee hearing there was evidence of the tension between the committee and the FCC. The first indication of tension was evidenced by who did and who did not attend the hearing. The eight witnesses who presented oral and written testimony to the committee represented both supporters and opponents of micro radio, each side supported by a technical radio engineer. Interestingly, the FCC commissioner who testified was not Chairman Kennard but rather Harold Furchtgott-Roth, a vocal opponent of the FCC's low-power initiative. NAB President Eddie Fritz testified as did representatives of the activist community, including the national coordinator of the Amherst Alliance Don Schellhardt and Virginia Tech professor and engineer, Ted Rappaport. Another high profile opponent of LPFM who testified was Kevin Klose, president and CEO of NPR. Basically the eight witnesses broke down along LPFM supporters and opponents, with each side represented by four people. A glance at the list revealed a notable absence of a significant LPFM proponent: FCC Chairman William Kennard. Commerce Committee Chairman William (Billy) Tauzin noted this absence in his opening remarks.

The champion of this new service, Chairman Kennard, was invited to join us this morning to discuss the merits. Because he has said so many times that this issue was one of his top priorities at the Commission, I had hoped he would accept the invitation. I even offered to postpone the hearing until noon that he might complete his public hearing today. Nonetheless, he declined because of commitments in Florida and that concerns me. (U.S. House Commerce Committee, 2000, pp. 2–3)

The FCC commissioner who did attend the hearing, Harold Furchtgott-Roth, was the only commissioner to vote against the LPFM initiative. Michael Powell, then a commissioner, dissented on a portion of the final "Report and Order" but Furchtgott-Roth was the only commissioner to completely oppose low-power radio. The only FCC official present at the hearing who supported LPFM was Deputy Chief of the Office of Engineering Bruce Franca.

The hearing consisted of each witness allotted five minutes for oral presentation of arguments, followed by a question and answer session by the assembled committee members. Committee Chairman Tauzin laid out the reason for the hearing in his opening remarks, drawing attention to the lack of respect given to the committee by the FCC as they moved ahead with the LPFM policy.

First and foremost, the FCC appears to have made a substantial public policy decision without seeking the advice and consultation of the Congress. The FCC is a quasi-independent agency of the U.S. Government, by law subject to Congress. Congress makes the policy that the FCC enforces. But with little regard for the opinions of the members of this committee, the Commission has now passed the final order creating these new low power radio licenses, even did so while we were out of session. (U.S. House Commerce Committee, 2000, p. 2)

Thus the battle lines were drawn and the struggle moved to a turf war over who had the authority to regulate the airwaves. Tauzin clearly felt slighted by the FCC process, despite a yearlong public comment period on the LPFM proposal by the FCC. The fact that Tauzin made this issue his "first and foremost" point indicated the size of the political rift created by the FCC's process.

The second point raised by Tauzin and the issue that became central to the entire debate as it moved through Congress was the question of interference. The FCC conducted their own research and attempted to balance the discrepancies among the other studies submitted. The mere fact that there were discrepancies became a central issue of concern for many of the congressional representatives who attempted to make sense of the technical issues. Committee Chairman Tauzin indicated his preconception when he stated:

It is clear to me—and I believe this hearing will only make it clearer—that the FCC's record on this matter does not support the conclusion that the newly created licenses will not interfere with other frequencies on the electromagnetic spectrum. (U.S. House Commerce Committee, 2000, p. 2)

Tauzin invoked the public interest in his defense of the status quo, questioning whether LPFM would be able to exist without causing unacceptable levels of interference:

I do not believe the Commission, as the manager of our Nation's electromagnetic spectrum, has adequately served the public interest when it proceeded to create these new licenses. . . . What we learn today will teach us a great deal about whether the Commission has acted precipitously, has acted without regard to the pubic interest, and whether the Congress needs to step in. (U.S. House Commerce Committee, 2000, pp. 2–3)

As the activist debate pointed out, the public interest could be invoked in defense of a wide range of positions. Here, the FCC was attacked for "acting without regard to the public interest" despite the vast majority of the 3,000 public comments supporting LPFM and the long list of public interest groups, churches, academics, and artists who supported the initiative.

Representative Michael Oxley (R-OH), the original sponsor of the Radio Broadcasting Preservation Act, followed Tauzin's comments. Oxley reiterated the concerns about interference and also raised concerns about how LPFM would affect the transition to digital radio. He also contested the FCC rule that allowed limited amnesty for some pirates: "I most object to the provisions making former unlicensed, pirate radio operators eligible for low power licenses, thus reinforcing their unlawful behavior and encouraging new unauthorized broadcasts in the future" (U.S. House Commerce Committee, 2000, p. 4). Oxley stated that he had initiated the legislation after radio station managers in his district expressed interference concerns, claiming that he had expressed his concerns to the FCC in writing and received no response, possibly adding to the tension between these government forces. He then acknowledged his intent to intervene if the FCC did not address his concerns: "By introducing the bill, I wanted to send the additional message that there were members who were prepared to act legislatively if the Commission's final rule did not adequately address the interference question" (U.S. House Commerce Committee, 2000, p. 4). Given the technical issues involved in determining what was "adequate," and the lack of technical expertise among the Congressional representatives, this appeared be a veiled threat where "adequate" was code for an outcome satisfactory to Oxley's constituents.

The opening volley ended with the ranking minority member of the subcommittee, Edward Markey (D) from Massachusetts. Markey acknowledged the potential of LPFM to increase diversity and expand opportunities for local community groups. Markey also praised the work of the FCC and noted the expansion of regulatory tasks they have undertaken without adding interference: broadcast, cellular, PCS, microwave, satellite, and so on. Markey said,

I want to applaud the Commission for exploring this worthwhile proposal and moving forward on it. The Commission is always at its best when it takes the public's airwaves resources and works to make more efficient use of that spectrum for the public. (U.S. House Commerce Committee, 2000, p. 5)

Thus the debate began to break down along partisan lines, with the Republicans challenging the policy of a Democrat-appointed FCC chairman and the Democratic representatives defending Kennard and LPFM. As the debate progressed, the party lines did not remain distinct and rhetoric of a "compromise" attracted members from both sides of the aisle to a position where politicians ultimately questioned FCC expertise.

The oral and written testimony from the witnesses followed familiar patterns, with NAB supporters contesting the FCC science that was used to establish acceptable levels of interference while micro radio supporters contested the NAB science. The definition of interference remained a sticking point, complicated by the committee members' attempt to simplify the debate and establish *either* increased interference or not. The committee members repeatedly pushed the radio engineers to state a position clearly, one way or the other. Because of a dispute over what measurement should be used to determine acceptable interference, signal-to-noise ratio or harmonic distortion, the engineers could not agree and their lack of consensus seemed to support the idea that more research was needed.

BIG WORDS AND INTERFERENCE

Beyond the expected positions articulated by the LPFM supporters and detractors, the testimony before the committee yielded two themes worthy of closer examination. First, NAB President Fritz and Commissioner Furchtgott-Roth used creative and dynamic language to discredit the entire premise of LPFM. These rhetorical flourishes are notable for their overt partisan nature and their patent disregard for the public input that contributed to the LPFM policy. Second, opponents of LPFM focused their criticism around the issue of interference. By making interference the primary concern, LPFM opponents were able to express their support for the concept of micro radio while they worked to dismantle this iteration of the policy. Interference then became a technocratic rational for opposing this public policy and a battleground where supporters and opponents could wage a numbers war.

Although the previous chapters of this research have revealed diverse rhetoric on the part of the activists, the hyperbole employed by NAB President Eddie Fritz in his testimony before the committee matched or exceeded the most extreme speech of the activists. Beginning by calling LPFM an "impending disaster," Fritz used the following contortion in an attempt to portray the crowded broadcast spectrum:

Let us put things in perspective. There are 12,000 radio stations licensed in the U.S. right now. To sort of get a grip on that, there are only 18,000 Burger King franchises in the world. (U.S. House Commerce Committee, 2000, p. 22)

That bit of illumination was followed by a long string of invective accusing the FCC of all manner of deceit:

Never before have I seen the FCC act with such willful disregard for Congress or to turn its back on the spectrum integrity they were trusted to oversee. . . . The FCC has abandoned its historic mission and really and truly forgotten the American consumer. (U.S. House Commerce Committee, 2000, p. 22)

Fritz may well have been correct when he said that the FCC had "forgotten the American consumer." Given the two models of the public interest outlined in Chapter 2, the FCC may have acted under the concept of the public sphere model as opposed to a marketplace model, thus turning consumers into citizens deserving more than the products deemed valuable by the logic of the marketplace.

Continuing to fuel the power struggle between the FCC and Congress, Fritz said, "I call this a rush to create interference before the Congress finds out about it" (U.S. House Commerce Committee, 2000, p. 22). Knowing the FCC was not going to yield to the demands of the NAB, Fritz emphasized the tension between Congress and the FCC in the hope that Congress would intervene on his behalf. To assert that Congress was not aware of LPFM after the widespread press coverage and extensive public comments about the issue can be interpreted as nothing more than a blatant attempt to enlist the Republican-led Congress to intervene in an otherwise enormously popular public policy initiative.

Given the NAB's active opposition to LPFM throughout the rulemaking process, Fritz's hyperbole was consistent with a level of rhetoric that denied the social need for, and the technical possibility of, licensing new low-power stations. This opposition was expected from the NAB. What was surprising was the use of similar language by an FCC commissioner.

Although he had voted against the LPFM proposal, the level of vitriol employed by Commissioner Furchtgott-Roth demonstrated a rhetorical slight of hand that actively masked particular virtues of the FCC's LPFM proposal. Given his privileged position within the FCC, Furchtgott-Roth had to have been aware of the nuances within the policy, yet his testimony was presented in such as way as to deny any benefits to micro radio and reinforce concerns about interference.

In my view, this action represents a severe incursion on the rights of current license holders, as well as on the value of those licenses. . . . This action impairs the ability of current licensees to serve their listeners, who must not be forgotten. (U.S. House Commerce Committee, 2000, p. 53)

Furchtgott-Roth went on to argue that FCC's goal of increasing diversity was greatly limited by the small number of stations that would be permitted in large urban areas. He stated that, because of congested airwaves, "no such stations would be created in New York, Los Angeles, Chicago, Philadelphia, San Diego, Dallas, San Francisco, Washington, Charlotte, and Miami" (U.S. House Commerce Committee, 2000, p. 53). This was true with regard to the 100-watt stations. What Furchtgott-Roth neglected to mention were the options for the smaller class of 10-watt stations. Applications for the smaller 10-watt class were not scheduled to be accepted until the 100-watt stations were established. By conflating the two, Furchtgott-Roth gave an inaccurate picture of the potential reach of LPFM.

The commissioner then argued that if the primary placement of LPFM stations was going to be rural areas, this was unnecessary because there were unfilled commercial frequencies in those locations. He also noted that because no one had applied for a low-power application prior to the FCC's new rule, there was no real public desire for the service. "There is no evidence in the behavior of actual license applicants that suggests any pent-up demand for the stations in question" (U.S. House Commerce Committee, 2000, p. 54). This statement was made without regard to the FCC's own statistics showing that they had received 13,000 inquires about low-power licenses prior to the LPFM rule.

HATE THE SIN, NOT THE SINNER

A consistent comment among the opponents of LPFM was their support for the policy but *not* the interference. Almost every opponent prefaced their remarks by supporting the idea of low-power radio but opposing this particular rule. Thus, interference became the central issue of debate, leaving behind many of the activist arguments about democracy, media consolidation, public access, and so on. This shift furthered the debate between the FCC and Congress while it sidestepped the bulk of the discourse generated by the activists. Examples of this qualified language include:

Committee Chair Tauzin said: "I appreciate, at least in principle, the notion that the FCC wishes to afford to churches, schools, civic organizations and other similarly situated groups a greater radio presence than they currently enjoy. However. . . . " (U.S. House Commerce Committee, 2000, p. 1)

NAB President Eddie Fritz said: "The FCC's goal of creating more diversity is laudable and we certainly support that, but this low power decision will not solve that problem." (U.S. House Commerce Committee, 2000, p. 23)

FCC Commissioner Furchtgott-Roth said: "At the outset of the low power proceeding, I made clear that I was not then and am not today opposed to the creation of a low power radio service per se. Whatever new service could have been provided within the range of existing interference regulations would have been worth considering." (U.S. House Commerce Committee, 2000, p. 52)

NPR President Klose said: "We favor in principle diversity of voices and access to the radio space. We acknowledge the intent of the FCC to expand diversity in adopting the recent report and order for a new service of low power radio stations to encourage such diversity. . . . However. . . . " (U.S. House Commerce Committee, 2000, p. 57)

These statements show the opponents of LPFM embracing the "laudable" "principle" of low-power radio while they worked to stop this specific low-power policy. The primary argument against LPFM was based on interference. Because the engineers presented different sets of data about interference and the committee members were not engineers, interference became a contested issue. Once contested, the interference issue allowed Republicans and Democrats alike to call for more study while they asserted their support for the concepts of LPFM. Thus, nontechnical politicians disputed the technical knowledge of the FCC and the complexity of interference allowed the committee members to vote in support of the Radio Broadcasting Preservation Act of 2000 and pass the legislation on to the full Congress. With interference established as the dominant issue, the congressional floor debate in the House would focus on the technical discourse instead of the larger social-political discourse generated by the activists.

CONGRESS LIMITS THE FCC: THE LANGUAGE OF COMPROMISE AMID GOVERNMENT STRUGGLE

On April 13, 2000, the U.S. House of Representatives voted on the Radio Broadcasting Preservation Act of 2000 (H.R. 3439, 2000) and the measure passed by a vote of 274 to 110 with 50 not voting (*Congressional Record*, 2000, p. H2318). Though a number of representatives made comments for and against the bill, using a range of ideas, two themes dominated the debate: The struggle between the FCC and Congress, and compromise. Thus the debate about LPFM, by the time it reached the floor of the House of Representatives, was largely portrayed as an intragovernmental struggle about who had the authority to regulate broadcasting. The majority answer to the resolution of this struggle was through the "compromise" embodied in the bill, allowing LPFM to move forward in a limited way while more interference studies could be conducted. The language and discourse of the activists was secondary to these other themes. Despite years of activism, thousands of comments submitted to the FCC and a nationwide coalition ranging from the AFL-CIO to the United Church of Christ, by the time Congress addressed the LPFM issue, it had been successfully reframed as a precipitous policy by a regulatory agency that circumvented Congress and in the process jeopardized the status quo of radio broadcasting.

Although the Commerce Committee hearing revealed tension between Congress and the FCC over the right to legalize low-power FM, it was during the House floor debate that that tension reached its nadir. In his opening statement, Representative Tauzin accused the FCC of illegally lobbying Congress on this issue by sending out a fax that listed ten reasons to support LPFM and oppose the Radio Broadcasting Preservation Act. This was said to be a criminal act, violating a law that prohibits government money from being used to promote partisan agendas. Tauzin said,

I intend to make a formal request upon the Department of Justice regarding a potential criminal violation of our statutes to the extent that the FCC, through its director and associate director of their political office has transmitted faxes . . . urging support or opposition to the bill that is before the house today. (*Congressional Record*, 2000, p. H2302)

Oxley followed and reiterated Tauzin's call for an investigation. As the author of the bill in question, Oxley was even more incensed by the FCC's attempt to rally congressional opposition to the bill. Oxley said,

This is something very, very serious when an independent agency can try to influence and ask for opposition to a particular piece of legislation.

But not only did they talk about the 10 reasons to oppose my bill, but then they added a letter from a labor union, the Federation of Labor and Congress of Industrial Organizations Legislative Alert, saying, "Oppose the Legislation. Oppose the Oxley Bill."

I do not think I can see any time in the 20 years I have been here a more blatant attempt to lobby this body by a so-called independent agency. It is an absolute outrage. I support the chairman for what he is trying to do in his referral to the Department of Justice. (*Congressional Record*, 2000, p. H2303)

As though this were not enough, Oxley went on to connect this to the moral development of our children. He extolled the virtues of not interfering in other people's business as he stood on the floor promoting legislation that would drastically interfere in the work of a regulatory agency. Oxley said,

Mr. Chairman, when we teach our children about good behavior, we teach them not to interfere with what other people are doing. We teach them not to step on other people's toes. And there is a lesson there for us today as we consider the direction of the low-power FM program. (*Congressional Record*, 2000, p. H2303)

The lesson in this case was to interfere in the technical work of a regulatory agency only when that work might compromise the profits of your campaign contributors. Despite the broadbased public support for LPFM, the commercial broadcasters via the NAB managed to convince a majority of congressional representatives that the FCC was promoting a policy that would undermine FM radio for everyone. Given the FCC's long history of conservative broadcast regulation, this was a serious charge, yet a charge that resonated enough to encourage the House of Representatives to hobble a significant public policy initiative.

Though nothing came of the Justice Department investigation, the charges of criminal behavior on the part of the FCC set the tone for the House debate. The question was moved from *if* Congress should respond to the LPFM rule to *how* Congress should respond. Initially, Oxley and others had hoped to stop all low-power licenses. After input from Democrats, Oxley conceded to a bill that would limit LPFM to licensing a few stations and a series of pilot studies to measure real world interference. Thus, the Radio Broadcasting Preservation Act of 2000 came to be seen as a compromise where the FCC was allowed to continue its program, though under the supervision of Congress.

Both Democratic and Republican House members throughout their comments on the floor used the language of compromise. Heather Wilson (R-NM), a member of the Commerce Committee said,

The idea of low-power radio is really kind of a neat idea that could open up radio to a lot more voices. So we have worked what I think is a good compromise in the committee. . . . I think this is a pretty good compromise. The FCC was moving too quickly and I believe compromising the quality of the radio reception that we get in our communities. (*Congressional Record*, 2000, pp. H2304–5)

Thus a compromise was needed to prevent compromised airwaves! Another Commerce Committee member, this time a Democrat, Frank Pallone, Jr. (D-NJ), agreed with the legislation and also characterized it as a compromise:

The compromise we fashioned in the Committee on Commerce allows the FCC to move forward with the low-power FM as long as it protects existing third-channel interference protections. The compromise then allows for an independent party to determine once and for all how these pilot programs will affect current radio listeners, small market broadcasters and blind radio reading services. The FCC will then report back to Congress in 2001. I think this compromise is a good one. (*Congressional Record*, 2000, p. H2305)

The language of compromise won the day as the House passed the legislation. There was opposition to the bill, primarily from Democrats; they *did* employ many of the concepts contained in the activist's, and later the FCC's, discourse. The familiarity of those arguments already described in this research alleviates the need to repeat the remarks of the House members who supported the FCC LPFM plan. Suffice it to say that the concepts that resulted in the creation of the LPFM policy were not enough to overcome the anxieties about interference produced by the dispute over which technical study to believe.

There was one attempt to limit congressional interference in FCC policy and that was the Barrett-Rush Amendment. This amendment would have accepted the Radio Broadcasting Preservation Act with one change: Congress would have six months to respond to the FCC once they submitted the results of the new interference tests. If Congress did not act within the six months, full regulatory authority would be restored to the FCC to implement LPFM. In promoting his amendment, Thomas Barrett (D-WI) acknowledged the uncertainty about interference and the ongoing questions about what study to believe:

This debate is really the legislative equivalent of, your mother wears army boots. We have had fights for the last several months between the proponents of low power radio and the opponents of low power radio. They are fighting over a study. The FCC does not like the study that has been prepared by the industry. The industry says that the FCC has not done a good enough job in studying this issue. So they go back and forth, back and forth, yelling at each other. (*Congressional Record*, 2000, p. H2311)

Barrett went on to outline what he saw as the disparity between the LPFM advocates and the commercial broadcasters. He saw his amendment as a way to return authority to the FCC and thus allow regulators, not politicians, to regulate the airwaves.

The reason why this amendment is important is because we do not have a level playing field here. On the one hand we have the radio stations, who have made it very, very clear that, regardless of the outcome of this study, they oppose having any type of expansion to low power FM stations.

On the other side we have the FCC, but the FCC really is speaking for groups that have no voice, by definition. They do not have radio stations. They do not have a powerful lobbying organization. They are the churches, the high schools, the neighborhood organizations.

What the bill does in its current form is it says even if this independent study comes back and says there are no interference problems, even if there are no interference problems, the FCC cannot continue to do the job it has done for the last 80 years, which is to make sure that the spectrum is filled in a fair way.

Instead, it says that Congress has to act first. I do not think there is a person in this room who believes that the opponents of low power FM radio are going to come back and say, okay, go ahead, change the law. (*Congressional Record*, 2000, pp. H2311–12)

Thus the supporters of LPFM *did* argue that the commercial broadcasters were using interference as a smokescreen to get LPFM out of the hands of the FCC and into a legislative process where their financial weight might work to their advantage. Nevertheless, the LPFM supporters were outnumbered and the House succeeded in passing the Radio Broadcasting Preservation Act of 2000.

The U.S. Senate was slow to act on this issue and did not hold open floor debates on a Senate version of the radio preservation act. The *Congressional Record* noted a series of statements submitted for the record in regard to the act. These statements included three letters all opposing LPFM. These letters came from Minnesota Public Radio, the International Association of Audio Information Services (IAAIS, often known as reading services for the blind), and the Minnesota State Services for the Blind. They all expressed concern about the interference that might be caused by LPFM and requested Senator Grams (R-MN) to support the LPFM revisions contained in the Radio Broadcasting Preservation Act of 2000.

RADIO BROADCASTING PRESERVATION ACT OF 2000: DEVIL IN THE DETAILS

The House Bill (H.R. 3439, 2000), introduce by Representative Michael Oxley (R) from Ohio and the Senate Bill (S. 3020, 2000), introduced by Senator Rod Gramms (R) from Minnesota contained similar language that was eventually inserted as a rider into the District of Columbia Appropriations Act, 2000 bill that President Clinton signed. This legislation directed the FCC to "revise its regulations authorizing the operation of new, low-power FM stations" (S. 3020). Though this bill did not completely stop the implementation of LPFM, major changes to the FCC decisions noted earlier were made.

The first significant change Congress made to the FCC LPFM rule was in regard to channel protection. The issue of how closely radio stations could be spaced on the radio dial without incurring interference was the subject of significant debate. The FCC decided to relax the standard of third adjacent channel protection and allow LPFM stations to occupy the frequencies located closer to existing broadcasters. Congress reversed this decision, reinstating the more conservative spacing standard and in the process, greatly reducing the number of possible frequencies available for low power stations.

The FCC shall modify the rules authorizing the operation of low power FM radio stations as proposed in MM Docket No. 99-25, to—

(A) prescribe minimum distance separations to third adjacent channels (as well as for co-channel and first- and second-adjacent channels). (S. 3020, 2000)

In addition, Congress added:

Congressional authority (is) required for further changes—The FCC may not—

(A) eliminate or reduce the minimum distance separations for third-adjacent channels. (S. 3020, 2000)

This intervention on FCC authority was followed by a rule reversing the decision to accept applications from pirates who had complied with FCC requests to stop illegal broadcasting. As noted earlier, the decision to allow *any* pirate to hold a broadcast license was hotly contested by the NAB and Congress apparently agreed and required the FCC to reverse this decision. Congress said the FCC must:

Prohibit any applicant from obtaining a low-power license if the applicant has engaged in any manner in the unlicensed operation of any station in violation of section of 301 of the Communications Act of 1934. (S. 3020, 2000)

The people who had advanced this issue through their grassroots activism were then eliminated from benefiting from their work.

Congress added a provision calling for a pilot study to add to the previous interference studies. This pilot program was intended to "further evaluate the need for third adjacent channel protection" (S. 3020, 2000). Congress wrote:

The Federal Communications Commission shall conduct an experimental program to test whether low-power FM radio stations will result in harmful interference to existing FM radio stations if such stations are not subject to the minimum distance separations for third-adjacent channels required by subsection (a). The Commission shall conduct such test in no more than nine FM radio markets, including urban, suburban, and rural markets, by waiving the minimum distance separations for third-adjacent channels for the stations that are the subject of the experimental program. (S. 3020, 2000)

This experiment to test for interference was then to be evaluated by an "independent testing entity." Given the existence of three interference studies all done with some partisan affiliation and a study by the FCC, Congress attempted to establish one unbiased source to evaluate interference levels. As the Rappaport study demonstrated, the ability to measure interference exceeded the ability of the human ear to perceive interference. The standards used to determine interference become a critical factor in determining the outcome of any study. Congress did not address this issue and merely mandated the FCC to designate an organization to conduct the study. What Congress *did* do, in an attempt to establish an objective measure, was allow for public comment on the interference and independent audience listening tests to determine "objectionable and harmful interference to the average radio listener" (S. 3020, 2000).

Finally, Congress mandated the FCC to report to Congress with the results of the interference study and the public reaction to the study and the pilot program. In addition, this report was to include an

evaluation of the impact of modification or elimination of minimum distance separations for third-adjacent channels on (i) listening audiences, (ii) incumbent FM broadcasters in general and minority and small market broadcasters in particular, including an analysis of the economic impact on such broadcasters, (iii) the transition to digital radio, (iv) stations that provide reading services to the blind and (v) FM radio translators. (S. 3020, 2000)

Despite the fact that the FCC had addressed these issues directly in their report, Congress called on the agency to reexamine these issues. The one significant difference between this Congressional mandate and the FCC rule was the requirement of the FCC to do an economic analysis of the impact of LPFM. No organization opposing LPFM made the overt argument about potential economic harm because that would mean the FCC was drafting policy based on market protectionism. Given the popularity of the neo-liberal model and the dominance or market forces as the supreme determinant of the shape and form of our social and material world, for the NAB to argue that LPFM would cause significant economic harm would not have been a persuasive argument to prevent the implementation of LPFM. Nevertheless, Congress added the economic analysis component to the review of LPFM, providing cover for those who had financial concerns though may have been unable to express them as a "legitmate" reason to limit LPFM.

Thus Congress duplicated the procedure the FCC had initiated throughout the previous two years. In overruling the work of the FCC and delaying the implementation of LPFM, Congress aided the position of the NAB and NPR while they delayed public access to a significant new media technology. There is a certain irony here when a body of democratically elected officials vote to overrule a regulatory agency. The commissioners of the FCC were not elected officials and thus not subject to the direct approval or disapproval of the U.S. voting public. Nevertheless, Kennard and his colleagues initiated one of the most significant public interest media policy initiatives in recent history during a period of unprecedented media consolidation and commercial domination. The irony then was that the elected officials in Congress, not the "faceless" bureaucrats at the FCC, acted to inhibit the LPFM initiative and pick up the industry discourse of interference protection. Although the FCC had employed an open public participation process that included an extended public comment period and extensive input from industry, activists, churches, educational organizations, civil rights groups, consumers rights groups, and more, Congress relied on one committee hearing in the House of Representatives and the anecdotal comments of those watchful groups who were aware of the legislation. Without so much as an open vote on the issue, LPFM was altered by attaching the Radio Broadcasting Preservation Act of 2000 to an appropriations bill to avoid a presidential veto. This could be seen as an inversion of the democratic process, where the officials elected to represent the public chose instead to represent the interests of the broadcast industry while the regulators at the FCC, often accused of regulating in the business interests, instead advanced the public interest.

Another perspective on this series of events is that the congressional legislation was nothing more than the display of raw political power on the part of the NAB. William Kennard was not an elected official; while this put him beyond the reach of the voting public, it also put him beyond the reach of the industry. Kennard was not reliant on the support (material or otherwise) of the NAB. For members of Congress, this was a different story. The financial and political might of the NAB has a long history as a political force in Washington and that force was brought to bear on the issue of LPFM. Though the congressional bill could not stand on its own, there was enough support to attach the legislation to the larger bill and force a signature from President Clinton. Aptly named, the Radio Broadcasting Preservation Act of 2000 did just that, preserved the status quo and delayed the most significant public interest broadcast policy in recent history. With the delay in place and a change of administration in 2001, the NAB effectively hobbled the new radio service for the time being.

Finally, the congressional intervention marks a weakness on the part of the media activism and reform movement to enlist legislative support for this issue. Though the movement had engaged in a wildly successful campaign of moving micro radio from the fringes of the radio dial to the policy books of the FCC, effective congressional lobbying remained outside the movement's grasp. Whether this was a testament to the influence of the power of money on the legislative process or a sign of a movement in need of maturation, delivering public sentiment to Congress proved no easy task. Without the benefit of a public comment period and an explicit legislative formation process, tracking the movement of individual bills and their supporters and opponents and then influencing those people individually proved beyond the ability of this nascent movement. Though the MRN listerv archive showed evidence of the activists' awareness of congressional action and the encouragement of letter and e-mail campaigns in opposition to the radio preservation act, either the volume or the content were not sufficient to persuade a majority to reject this legislation. Given the limitations of the *Congressional Record* for containing a smoking gun—evidence that congressional representatives were acting on behalf of the NAB—one can only speculate that the financial and political muscle of the micro radio community proved to be no match for the campaign contributions of the NAB. After years of struggle and strategy based around the FCC, Congress presented a new set of problems for the activists who were clearly outgunned by the NAB with its long history of congressional lobbying. Although beyond the scope of this study, future research could include interviews with congressional supporters and opponents of the Radio Broadcasting Preservation Act of 2000 to try to determine the larger motivations behind the legislation. Political decisions are always mired with contradictions though in this case, the activists and the press saw this vote as a display of raw power on the part of the commercial broadcasters and another indication of the corrupting influence of wealth and power on our democratic system.

Conclusion: Re-Cognizing
Media and a Movement

This research on the struggle over micro radio reveals not only a coordinated effort to reestablish community radio stations, but also demonstrates the active presence of a diverse movement seeking to reconceptualize the role of media in society. Micro radio provided an opportunity for the media activism and reform movement to publicly display a powerful set of ideas about the relationship of access to media and a functioning democracy. This knowledge was displayed through grassroots activism such as illegal micro broadcasting and colorful protest demonstrations. The ideas behind micro radio were also displayed in more traditional, institutional settings such as courtrooms and newspapers. The academic community published and spoke about this issue, providing invaluable historical, political and economic accounts of the issues embodied in micro radio as well as an element of legitimacy to many of the claims made by activists.

The combined efforts of grassroots, institutional, and academic theories and practices—cognitive terrain and cognitive praxis—helped move micro radio from the housing projects of Illinois to the pages of the *Federal Register*. In the process, the larger issues of public access to media technology and the influence of media consolidation received renewed attention from politicians and the public alike. Although the relationship between media and democracy may still not be thoroughly integrated into common conceptions of everyday life, the micro radio issue became an influential site where concrete examples of the power and potential of local, public access community media were demonstrated.

EXPLORING COGNITIVE TERRAIN: ACTIVISTS' ON-LINE DEBATES

This research corroborated Coopman's (2000a, b) research on the importance of the Internet to the micro radio activists. Chapters 2 and 3 contained detailed examinations of the actual dialogue that took place on-line, providing a unique historical glimpse into the movement's discursive practices. The listserv archive captured a national dialogue among group leaders and participants from a range of ideological and institutional perspectives. Examining the on-line discussions allowed for an intimate look at the experimentation that goes into the process of exploring a new cognitive terrain. As the media activism and reform movement attempted to develop a set of coherent strategies and core principles, the activists encountered the messy details of life. The contingent, historically specific and contradictory nature of concepts such as "the public interest" and "commercialism" proved difficult to readily enlist in the service of micro radio. The process of debating the value of the concept of "the public interest" yielded historical references to previous broadcast regulation as well as connections to academic discourses that have critiqued the public interest standard throughout the history of broadcast regulation.

The MRN listserv debates (Chapter 2) can be seen as examples of "cosmology formation." Eyerman and Jamison (1991) argued that every social movement relied on a set of "worldview assumptions, attitudes toward nature and society" (p. 70). The listserv debates show the activists working through two of the issues that fit into a larger "worldview" about the nature of the media in general and micro radio in particular. "Cosmology formation is a kind of translation process, translating terms from an internal scientific discourse to public space, to social and political action" (Eyerman & Jamison, 1991, p. 71). Thus, for the idea of the public interest to be useful to the micro radio activists, a demonstration of what public interest micro radio might actually *sound* like was necessary. Similarly, the limitations imposed by a commercial ban on micro radio gained serious attention when they were grounded in the actual experiences of a micro broadcaster attempting to keep a station on the air. The ideas needed to be put into practice as well as argued about theoretically. The social movement behind micro radio provided the cognitive space (technical information, philosophy, and enthusiasm) for the exploration of theoretical and practical applications of public interest and (non)commercial broadcasting.

In much the same way that this study provided examples of activists struggling to develop a "cosmology" (Chapter 2), this study also provides two examples of the activists' struggle to identify "the Other" (Chapter 3). The identification of the specific forces opposing the goals of a movement is a significant part of the process of social change. In the case of micro radio, initially the FCC and the commercial broadcasters represented by the NAB were easily identified "Others," forces opposing micro radio. Two groups that proved more difficult to identify and respond to were the Christian community and National Public Radio (NPR). On one hand, segments of the Christian community were contributing micro radio activists, going on-air illegally in search of local contact with their congregations. On the other hand, large Christian organizations such as the American Family Association (AFA), which already owned significant numbers of radio and television stations, opposed micro radio. Also, some of the activists feared that groups like the AFA, with their nonprofit status, would grab up low-power licenses and operate what amounted to a national network of local chapters. As it turned out, the FCC rule included a number of provisions that would prohibit such a scenario. For the activists on the MRN listserv struggling to determine the potential impact of the Christian community, this outcome was not predetermined. The Christian community became a complex group to assign a label of "Other" to and the MRN community remained divided as to how to respond to the Christian involvement in micro radio.

NPR, with their stated opposition to micro radio, proved to be more easily identified as "Other," though the strategies and tactics for responding to NPR caused considerable debate among MRN subscribers. The assumption that NPR would support the expansion of public radio was quickly refuted as NPR joined the NAB in opposing the FCC plan to license low-power FM. The activists responded to this news with a range of opinions, though most felt betrayed by a potentially influential ally. Many activists also supported their local public radio stations and were reluctant to punish those stations over the decisions of the national NPR board. Again, the activists were forced to distinguish "the Other" from the allies, in this case, the local from the national.

The struggle to define the opposition within NPR and the Christian community was connected to the larger issue of struggle against the media conglomerates that dominated the airwaves. In both the NPR and Christian cases, the bulk of the opposition came from large, centrally organized, well-financed groups seeking to protect their respective pieces of the broadcast spectrum. In some cases the local representatives of these groups supported the national agenda, although more often the local church or NPR affiliate was in support of micro radio. Sifting through the networks of power that determined the positions and influence of NPR and the Christian community required active work on the part of micro radio activists. This work within a social movement often goes unseen. The MRN provided a historical record of that work and the difficulties faced in determining "the Other."

From this diverse struggle over media and democracy, some lessons emerge. First, the success of the micro radio activists in moving their issues from a fringe concern to a policy initiative at the FCC can be attributed a combination of persistence and coordination. McChesney and Nichols (2002b) affirmed this conclusion when they wrote: "The microradio fight illustrates the enormous potential of a well-organized reform movement" (p. 41). The effort to legalize LPFM took place over the course of a decade with mounting activism as time passed. Illegal stations appeared all across the United States in the late 1990s, making enforcement increasingly difficult and expensive for the FCC. At the same time, diverse groups were united behind the concept of LPFM, creating a large, politically heterogeneous constituency that could not be ignored. From the National Lawyers Guild to the United Church of Christ, civic, religious, and community groups supported the idea of community radio. By building this diverse coalition, the activists promoted the ideas behind LPFM while they created a support base with political muscle. Thus the proposed typology of the media activism and reform movement reflects the diversity of the micro radio activists and reinforces the necessity of uniting diverse political and social skill sets in the service of a movement. Grassroots activism without the historical knowledge of academic scholars is sure to fail. Similarly, policy institutions need grassroots action to initiate media coverage, gain public attention, and move issues beyond the pages of journals and position papers. This movement demonstrated the interdependence of activism, policy, and scholarship.

MICRO RADIO IN THE NEWS

The news media played a significant role in the promotion of micro radio. In the examination of the dominant newspaper coverage of micro radio, a steady increase in the amount of coverage was found, coupled with a primarily favorable framing that resulted in widespread distribution of the arguments supporting the proliferation of micro radio. The newspaper coverage provided a public forum for the activists, allowing micro broadcasters to make their case as to why local media was important. This news coverage showed the pirates to be more than hobbyists or anarchists out to make trouble. Instead, the newspaper coverage drew on familiar metaphors to tell the story of David and Goliath. The familiar media metaphors worked to the activists' advantage, allowing the newspapers to use a form of cultural shorthand to convey the idea that the small and oppressed were fighting a battle of justice against the large, powerful oppressors. Although in many ways the coverage relied on familiar news values, metaphors, and sources, these all tended to work in favor of the activists and against the wishes of the NAB.

One of the news production patterns that worked to the micro broadcasters' advantage was story structure. Many of the stories during the three years of coverage began with the individual case of a broadcaster and his/her struggle with the FCC. The coverage of the grassroots activity within the movement provided grounded details about a specific person or group usually working within the community where the newspaper was based. This first-hand account of people struggling to gain access to radio brought the large, theoretical ideas of the media activism movement down to a level where a local reader could find those ideas applied on the radio dial. In contrast to the pirates, the NAB representatives was often quoted from the national office or at best, a representative of a state branch of the NAB. In a few cases, local radio station owners were quoted about their interference concerns, although the majority of coverage relied on quotes from NAB headquarters to refute the assertions of the micro broadcasters. In effect, this gave the activists a home court advantage, allowing reporters to speak directly with the pirates and experience the broadcasts firsthand. In most cases the NAB didn't have the tangible demonstration of local interference and thus their arguments against micro radio remained more abstract, posing hypothetical interference against a station that was already on the air (illegally).

Having grounded the ideas behind micro radio activism in the case of a local pirate, newspaper stories typically then turned to authorities to support or contradict the activists' contentions. In most cases, this space was filled by representatives from the institutional component of the media activism and reform movement. The Media Access Project and the National Lawyers Guild were often cited, giving contextual information about the patterns of broadcast ownership and the effects of media consolidation. These quotes reflect the cultural capital embodied in these more formal institutions and demonstrate the valuable role these institutions play in advancing the cognitive terrain of a movement.

A major component to almost every newspaper story was quotations from the FCC. The FCC, and Chairman Kennard in particular, initially framed as a prosecutor of illegal pirates, eventually came to be *the* spokesman *for* micro radio. Kennard used strong language in support of micro radio in many of his speeches and interviews and these powerful phrases made their way into the newspaper coverage, often supplanting the voices of the activists. In some respects, Kennard's enthusiastic promotion of LPFM was a major success for the activists and furthered the dominant cause of micro radio. In another sense, Kennard homogenized a heterogeneous movement and repeatedly called on the need for "churches and schools" to have access to the radio, although activists' conception of the range of groups hoping for access to the airwaves exceeded the traditional nonprofit groups that already existed in many communities. In following the familiar news production pattern of reliance on official sources and enduring news values, the newspapers relied on Kennard to sell micro radio and in the process, painted a generic picture of potential new broadcasters that effaced the eclectic groups that had initiated the micro crusade. In one sense, the result of Kennard's support was a form of co-optation, where movement ideas were brought into a mainstream institution and in the process reconfigured in such a way as to severely limit the power and potential of those ideas.

The media coverage of micro radio raises a question for micro radio advocates and the larger movement: How can public support for community media be built? The public is notably absent from the struggle over micro radio. The lack of broadbased public support may have facilitated the congressional intervention into LPFM and allowed for a political process that favored vested interests over public access. Although the micro radio activists aggressively debated the "public interest," they failed to actively debate *how* to enlist public support for micro radio. The public remained an untapped resource for the activists, in part due to the complexity and difficulty of explaining the significance of micro radio to the uninitiated. The issue of widespread public support for micro radio remains an area in need of attention if micro radio and media activism is to achieve the level of public awareness afforded other movements such as environmentalism. Without public support for access to communication technology, micro radio and media activism will likely remain within the province of academics and special interest activists. Given the level of media saturation in the United States (albeit dominated by the global media conglomerates), raising public awareness about the value of community media is no small task, though it is integral to the future success of micro radio and media activism in general.

ACTIVISM AND FCC POLICY

The FCC "Report and Order" that created the low-power radio service is a map of many of the discourses generated by micro radio activists. Throughout this eighty-page document, major contributors to both the MRN listserv and the micro radio project in general are cited to support the position chosen by the FCC. The presence of these organizations in one of the most significant public broadcasting policy initiatives in decades was a testament to the combined efforts of the grass-roots activists, the policy and legal institutions, and the academic researchers who laid the ground work and actively supported micro radio. In a period of unprecedented media consolidation amid a dominant discourse of neo-liberal market ideology, the combined forces of the media activism and reform movement succeeded in helping to convince the chairman of the FCC and three other commissioners to vote to license low-power community radio after a twenty-year hiatus. The evidence that the FCC was listening to the activists resides in the LPFM 'Report and Order," where activist organizations are cited repeatedly.

The FCC's decisions with regard to LPFM adds a cultural component to McChesney's model of how the FCC operates. McChesney has argued that the FCC is a regulatory agency beholden to the industry. This classic political economic perspective posits that the FCC is controlled by the economic forces behind the NAB, the same group that determines the shape of the political landscape through their contributions to members of Congress. In the case of micro radio, we saw FCC Chairman Kennard contradict the NAB repeatedly to the point of accusing the commercial broadcasters of spreading false information in their bid to kill LPFM. Thus, the regulatory agency did not appear beholden to the broadcast industry. Instead, the regulatory agency, insulated from the need for campaign donations, challenged the NAB and initiated policy that was largely intended to support local, small-scale, nonprofit media making. Though the FCC's LPFM plan was not everything the activists wanted, it would be difficult to see this policy as a product of industry desire by an agency beholden to that industry. The LPFM policy was in many ways the direct result of cultural activism initiated and maintained by the movement this book attempts to identify and describe.

With the evisceration of the FCC's LPFM plan through congressional passage of the Radio Broadcasting Preservation Act of 2000, the question of political economic influence on the U.S. government takes on a larger scope. The LPFM case suggests an opening in the landscape of how regulation happens. In this case, the nonelected commissioners of the FCC supported a major new public service initiative. In response, the elected members of Congress voted to overturn an initiative designed to benefit their voters. The legislation Congress passed instead supported the broadcast industry. This could be seen as an inversion of the democratic process, where the appointed officials promoted the rights of the general public while the popularly elected representatives voted to support their contributors over their constituents. With a cynically titled bill masking the intent to limit the implementation of micro radio, this bill never received a full and fair hearing by Congress or the American people and instead was attached as a rider to another bill through political maneuvering. Although it is easy to take a cynical view of the motivations of regulators at the FCC, it is more frightening to think the congressional process can be so easily bought by the rich and powerful. The case of LPFM raises questions about the possibility for reform in the FCC, and in turn raises larger questions about the strength of democracy in the United States at the turn of the millennium. Since leaving the FCC, Kennard has remained quiet about limits placed on his work to advance micro radio as a public policy. Recently, McChesney interviewed Kennard for *The Nation* and used the former FCC Chair's comments to critique the current Bush administration's plans for broadcast regulation. Describing the LPFM debacle, McChesney wrote: "Kennard's inability to advance even a very modest public service agenda is a good indication of the corruption of communications policy-making today. And indications are that matter will only get worse under the Bush administration" (McChesney, 2001, p. 17). In this article, Kennard is described as frustrated by his inability to offset the effects of media consolidation and enact policies that promoted the public interest. Kennard confirmed the discourse of the media activism and reform movement, acknowledging the power of the media to shape how we think about the world when he said:

"These broadcast licenses are not widgets. They impact the way people think, the way our children learn, the way people get information about politics in the public process, and I've always believed it's vitally important that there be a multiplicity of outlets for expression." . . . Kennard said progressives should pay close attention to the FCC, because "even though it is almost an invisible government agency, it plays a vitally important role in how people live their day-to-day lives and how our democracy functions." (McChesney, 2001, pp. 17–20)

Thus Kennard echoed the core tenets of the media activism and reform movement. The micro radio issue drew attention to the FCC, pointing to the need for local access media.

Unlike the influential Telecommunications Act of 1996 that received very little media coverage yet was responsible for reconfiguring broadcast regulation, micro radio activists were able to draw grassroots, institutional, academic, and public attention to *one* small piece of FCC policy: the LPFM initiative. As the first major foray into the realm of re-cognizing the role of media in the information age, the micro radio issue demonstrated the breadth and depth of the media activism and reform movement and moved media regulatory policy from the pages of journals and onto the front pages of newspapers.

Another sign of the integration of the knowledge generated by the media activism and reform movement comes in the form of pedagogical promotion. In the latest edition of a popular mass communication text book (Campbell, Martin, & Fabos, 2001), micro radio and the case of Stephen Dunifer are cited under the heading "Radio, Ownership and Democracy." This chapter segment summarizes the changes wrought by media consolidation, leaving students with the following question:

With a few large broadcast companies now permitted to dominate radio ownership nationwide, will this consolidation of power in any way restrict the number and kinds of voices permitted to speak over the public airwaves? To ensure that mass-media industries continue to serve democracy, the public needs to play a role in developing the answer to this question. (Campbell, Martin, & Fabos, 2001, p. 131)

In a veiled way, this textbook encourages students to take up the cause of the media activism and reform movement and participate in the process of media regulation. Prior to the 2001 edition, this and many other university-level mass communication texts failed to mention the struggle over micro radio. The integration of micro radio into standard pedagogical practice is yet another indication of the movement's success at integrating ideas about media and democracy into the forms and practices of everyday life.

MICRO RADIO, MEDIA ACTIVISM: NOW WHAT?

As of March 2004, the whole story of micro radio has not been told. The FCC has begun the process of issuing licenses to stations that meet the more stringent requirements of the Congressional legislation. Also, Senator John McCain (R-AZ) has proposed legislation that would overturn the Radio Broadcasting Preservation Act of 2000 and restore full broadcast regulatory authority to the FCC. Thus, the actual implementation of micro radio policy is far from complete, and a diverse activist community is watching to see if further civil disobedience and movement activity is needed to keep this issue alive. Also, the new FCC Chairman Michael Powell has not demonstrated a commitment to LPFM despite his initial vote in favor of the policy. Seventy-three stations have received licenses to broadcast under the new LPFM policy, a far cry from the thousands imagined by the activists and far fewer than the number of illegal stations still in operation. A rough breakdown of the groups receiving licenses reveals about a third (twenty-seven) of the groups as religious organizations, seventeen schools or educational organizations, seven city based groups and twenty-two groups with an unknown emphasis. This brief overview calls for further scholarship in this area. The details of the emerging micro radio policy offer excellent potential future research opportunities as citizens begin to gain renewed access to an old technology. Who ends up with licenses and what they chose to broadcast are significant questions that deserve scholarly attention as this issue moves forward.

This research covered a small segment of a large, complex social issue. Further detailed ethnographic research of the micro broadcasters and the content of their programming would offer insight into the potential contributions of community media. Similarly, further exploration of the larger media activism and reform movement could include critical profiles of the many groups who address questions of media reform. Identifying the goals, tactics, and strategies of this multifaceted movement would begin to reveal the breadth and depth of work taking place under the rubric of media activism. As further study of media activism emerges, effective parallels to other social movements may point to pathways that facilitate the distribution of movement knowledge beyond the confines of a special interest group.

Regardless of the outcome of the ongoing struggle over micro radio, a larger question remains about the rise and influence of media activism as a social movement. Like the environmental movement that is never finished protecting wildlife or clean air and water, the emerging media activism and reform movement will need to continue to work for issues of media and democracy, free communications and access to media technology. The micro radio issue provided an opportunity for many people to experience first hand the impact of diverse, accessible radio. This tangible learning reinforced and reinvigorated the dry, abstract work of policy wonks and academics that too often remains inaccessible to the public. Connecting the tangible to the theoretical was part of the mapping of the cognitive terrain that took place around the micro radio issue. This mapping included experimenting with technologies and discursive concepts, trial and error, exploring the difficulties of hiding a signal from the FCC or agreeing on the meaning of the public interest. This was the cognitive praxis that coalesced around micro radio, repeated through the news media and translated into government policy.

Although the micro radio issue received significant attention from the FCC, widespread popular understanding of the issue remains limited. This raises the question of whether media activism is actually at the level of a widespread social movement or rather still in the formative stages, a proto-movement if you will. The knowledge about media that resides and circulates within the grassroots, institutional, and academic communities gained a degree of public exposure through the issue of micro radio, although micro radio continues to be a phrase that elicits looks of confusion from many people. In many ways, media activism has yet to experience a critical juncture such as what Carson's *Silent Spring* achieved for the environmental movement. The lack of a high-profile, popular text and or media event that encapsulates the ideas and agendas of the media activism and reform movement is a significant impediment to the circulation of the knowledge promoted by this movement.

Scholars continue to research the many-faceted relationships between media and society; policy institutions monitor and critique the public and private media sectors; and grassroots activists broadcast illegally. Yet concerns about the media have yet to stir the popular imagination into action to the level seen in other movements. Despite a vigorous campaign to legalize low-power FM, for the moment, media activism remains a proto-movement—a movement rich with theory and practice yet lacking the broad based popular understanding and support that could result in systemic changes to a consolidated media system.

Although the micro radio issue suffered a setback from the congressional action, the possibilities for new community radio remain viable. On one hand, the Republican domination of national politics in the United States will likely slow any further public interest initiatives in the realm of telecommunications policy. Republicans have consistently rejected market interference and promoted policies that facilitate media ownership consolidation. On the other hand, the micro radio activists established a coordinated network of affinity groups who are now looking at the issue of community media. This advocacy block will continue to exert pressure on regulators and politicians. In addition, the implementation of the first round of low-power stations, coupled with the "test stations" in nine markets as mandated by Congress, will all be reviewed at some point and depending on the congressional make-up at that time, the FCC may be allowed to implement LPFM as they originally envisioned. Thus, micro radio will continue to be a policy issue that embodies a critique of deregulated telecommunications policy.

Many other fronts remain on the media activism horizon: media literacy, media criticism, news watch and analysis, defense of public resources in the broadcast spectrum during the expansion of wireless communication, universal access to digital technology to overcome the many manifestations of the digital divide, and more. These are some of the issues being addressed by other facets of the media activism and reform movement. Like micro radio, many of these issues will require historically specific events to allow the issue to reach the public consciousness in a meaningful and influential way. In the meantime, the movement connections established by the micro radio struggle may yield a more vigorous and broadbased reaction to the issues of media and democracy. Given the scope and influence of our information society, access to the means of cultural production and distribution (media technology) will continue to be a central component of a functioning democracy. Information and the power of representation drive our conceptions of the world. It is only through a vibrant, diverse marketplace of ideas that the best ideas can emerge. This is the central message of the media activism and reform movement, a movement that has just begun to reshape our conceptions of the role of media in a democratic society.

Bibliography

Atton, C. (2001). *Alternative media*. London: Sage Publications.

Aufderheide, P. (2000). *The daily planet: A critic on the capitalist culture beat*. Minneapolis: University of Minnesota Press.

———. (1999). *Communications policy and the public interest: The telecommunications act of 1996*. New York: Guilford Press.

Barlow, W. (1988). Community radio in the U.S.: The struggle for a democratic medium. *Media, Culture and Society*, 81(101).

Benton Foundation (1998, April). What's local about local broadcasting. Available on-line at www.benton.org/Television/whatslocal.html.

Campbell, R., Martin, C. R., & Fabos, B. (2001). *Media and culture: An introduction to mass communication*. New York: Bedford/St. Martin's.

Chouliaraki, L., & Fairclough, N. (1999). *Discourse in late modernity: Rethinking critical discourse analysis*. Edinburgh: Edinburgh University Press.

Cockburn, A. C. (1997, December 15). Free radio, crazy cops, and broken windows. *The Nation*. Available on-line at www.radio4all.org/news/cockburn.html.

Communications Act of 1934, 48 Stat. 1064 (1934).

Congressional Record. (2000). 104th Cong., 2nd sess. April 13, 2000 (House), pp. H2302–H2318. From the *Congressional Record*. Available on-line at wais.access.gpo.gov.

Coopman, T. M. (2000a). Hardware handshake: Listserv forms backbone of national free radio network. *American Communication Journal*, 3(3). Available on-line at www.acjournal.org.

———. (2000b). High speed access: Micro radio, action, and activism on the internet. *American Communication Journal*, 3(3). Available on-line at www.acjournal.org.

———. (1999). Defining public interest in the micro radio debate: Canadian v. U.S. policies. Western States Communication Association Convention, Vancouver, BC, 1999.

———. (1998). Free radio v. the FCC: A case study of micro broadcasting. National Communication Association Convention, Mass Communication Division, Chicago, 1997.

———. (1997). Pirates to micro broadcasters: The rise of the micro radio movement. Western States Communication Association Convention, Monterey, CA, 1997.

———. (1995). Sailing the spectrum from pirates to micro broadcasters: A case study of micro broadcasting in the San Francisco bay area. Master's Thesis.

Couldry, N. (2000). *The place of media power: Pilgrims and witnesses of the media age*. London: Routledge.

Croteau, D., & Hoynes, W. (2001). *The business of media: Corporate media and the public interest*. London: Pine Forge Press.

Dagron, A. G. (2001). *Making waves: Stories of participatory communication for social change*. New York: Rockefeller Foundation.

Dick, S. J., & McDowell, W. (2001). From pirates to public service: The saga of LPFM. Popular Communication Conference, Radio Studies Division, Philadelphia.

———. (2000). Pirates, pranksters, and prophets: Understanding America's unlicensed "free" radio movement. *Journal of Radio Studies*, 7(2), pp. 329–341.

Downing, J.D.H. (2003). The IMC movement beyond "the West." In *Representing resistance: Media, civil disobedience, and the global justice movement*. Andy Opel and Donnalyn Pompper, eds. Westport, CT: Praeger.

———. (2001). *Radical media: Rebellious communication and social movements*. London: Sage.

Drew, J. (1995). Media activism and radical democracy. In *Resisting the virtual life: The culture and politics of information*. James Brooks and Ian A. Boal, eds. San Francisco: City Lights Books.

Edmondson, R. (2000). *Rising up: Class warfare in America from the streets to the airwaves*. San Francisco: Librad Press.

Escobar, A. (1992). Culture, economics, and politics in Latin American social movements theory and research. In *The making of social movements in Latin America*. A. Escobar and S. E. Alvarez, eds. Boulder, CO: Westview Press.

Eyerman, R., & Jamison, A. (1991). *Social movements: A cognitive approach*. State College: Penn State Press.

FAIR (Fairness and Accuracy in Reporting). (2000, October 19). "Democracy now!" in danger: Pacifica turns against free speech. Available on-line at www.fair.org.

Fairchild, C. (2001). *Community radio and public culture*. Cresskill, NJ: The Hampton Press.

Fairclough, N. (1995). *Critical discourse analysis: The critical study of language*. London: Longman.

———. (1992). *Discourse and social change*. Cambridge: Polity Press.

FCC (2000). Creation of a Low Power Radio Service, MM Docket No. 99-25, FCC (proposed January 20, 2000). Report and Order.

———. (1999). Creation of a Low Power Radio Service, MM Docket No. 99-25, FCC (proposed January 28, 1999). Available on-line at www.fcc.gov/Bureaus/Mass_Media/Notices/1999/fcc99006.txt, Notice of Proposed Rulemaking.

————. (1978). Changes and Rules to Noncommercial Educational FM Broadcast Stations, 69 F.C.C. 2d 240.

Ferguson, S. (1998, May 19). Rebel radio. *The Village Voice*, p. 63.

Fornatale, P., & Mills, J. (1980). *Radio in the television age*. Woodstock, NY: Overlook Press.

Foucault, M. (1977). *Discipline and punish: The birth of the prison*. New York: Pantheon.

Fowler, R. (1991). *Language in the news: Discourse and ideology in the press*. London: Routledge.

Franck, Peter, Esq. (1998). Broadcasting, the constitution and democracy. Position paper, National Lawyers Guild Committee on Democratic Communications, presented to the National Association of Broadcasters, Las Vegas, April 6, 1998.

Free Speech v. FCC (1998, May 12). 98 Civ. 2680 (MBM), First Amended Complaint.

Gans, H. J. (1979). *Deciding what's news: A study of "CBS Evening News," "NBC Nightly News,"* Newsweek *and* Time. New York: Pantheon.

Gitlin, T. (1980). *The whole world is watching: Mass media in the making and unmaking of the new left*. Berkeley: University of California Press.

Habermas, J. (1989). *The structural transformation of the public sphere*. Cambridge: MIT Press.

Hackett, R. (2000). Taking back the media: Notes on the potential for a communicative democracy movement. *Studies in Political Economy*, 63(Autumn 2000), pp. 61–86.

Halleck, D. (2001). *Handheld visions*. New York: Fordham University Press.

Hamelink, C. (1995). *World communication: Disempowerment and self-empowerment*. London: Zed Books.

Hamilton, J. (2000). Alternative media: Conceptual difficulties, critical possibilities. *Journal of Communication Inquiry*, 24(4), pp. 357–371.

Harvey, D. (1996). *Justice, nature and the geography of difference*. Oxford: Blackwell.

————. (1990). *The condition of postmodernity*. Malden, MA: Blackwell.

Hazen, D., & Winokur, J. (1997). *We the media: A citizen's guide to fighting for media and democracy*. New York: The New Press.

Held, D, (1996). *Models of democracy*. Stanford: Stanford University Press.

Henry, S., & von Joel, M. (1984). *Pirate radio: Then and now*. New York: Sterling Publishing.

Herman, E. S., & McChesney, R. W. (1997). *The global media: The new missionaries of global capitalism*. Washington, DC: Cassell.

Hornblower, M. (1998, April 20). Radio free America. *Time*, 151, 4.

Howley, K. H. (2000). Radiocracy rulz: Microradio as electronic activism. *International Journal of Cultural Studies*, 3(2), pp. 256–267.

————. (1999). Community media and cultural studies: Recommendations for a research agenda. Researching Culture Conference, London, 1999.

Jassem, H. (2000) American pirate radio: The new local radio? International Communication Association Conference, Acapulco, Mexico, 2000.

Jones, Steve. (1994). Unlicensed broadcasting: content and conformity. *Journalism Quarterly*, 71, pp. 395–402.

Karliner, J. (1997). *The corporate planet: Ecology and politics in the age of globalization*. San Francisco: Sierra Club Books.

Kennard, William. (1998a, August 9) National Public Radio interview. Available on-line at www.radio4all.org/news/kennard-npr.html.

————. (1998b, October 16). Remarks to National Association of Broadcasters Convention, Seattle, 1998.

Kidd, D. (2003). Become the media: The global IMC network. In *Representing resistance: Media, civil disobedience, and the global justice movement*. Andy Opel and Donnalyn Pompper, eds. Westport, CT: Praeger.

Korn, A. (1996). Micro radio vs. the FCC: The case of Stephen Dunifer and Free Radio Berkeley. *National Lawyers Guild Practitioner*, 53.

Krasnow, E. G., & Longley, L. D. (1978). *The politics of broadcast regulation*. New York: St. Martin's Press.

Labaton, S. (1999, January 9). F.C.C. offers low-power FM stations. *New York Times*, C1.

Ledbetter, J. (1997). *Made possible by: The death of public broadcasting in the United States*. New York: Verso.

McChesney, R. W. (2001, May 14). Kennard, the public and the FCC. *The Nation*, pp. 17–20.

————. (1999). Rich media poor democracy: Communication politics in dubious times. Chicago: University of Illinois Press.

————. (1998). The political economy of radio. In *Seizing the airwaves: A free radio handbook*. R. Sakolsky and S. Dunifer, eds. San Francisco: AK Press.

————. (1997). *Corporate media and the threat to democracy*. New York: Seven Stories Press.

————. (1993). Telecommunications, mass media, and democracy: The battle for the control of U.S. broadcasting, 1928–1935. New York: Oxford University Press.

————. (1988). Franklin Roosevelt, his administration and the Communications Act of 1934. *American Journalism*, 5, 304–309.

McChesney, R. W., & Nichols, J. (2002a, January 7/14). The making of a movement: Getting serious about media reform. *The Nation*, pp. 11–17.

————. (2002b). *Our media not theirs: The democratic struggle against corporate media*. New York: Seven Stories Press.

Melucci, A. (1989). New perspectives on social movements: An interview with Alberto Melucci. In A. Melucci, *Nomads of the present: Social movements and individual needs in contemporary society*. Philadelphia: Temple University Press.

Mosco, V. (1996). *Then political economy of communication: Rethinking and renewel*. London: Sage.

Negroponte, N. (1995). *Being digital*. New York: Alfred A. Knopf.

Olien, C. N., Tichnor, P.J., & Donohue, G. A. (1989). Media coverage and social movements. In *Information Campaigns: Balancing social forces and social change*. C. T. Solomon, ed. London: Sage.

Phillips, P. (1999). *The progressive guide to alternative media and activism*. New York: Seven Stories Press.

Phipps, Steven P. (1991). Unlicensed broadcasting and the federal radio commission: The 1930 George W. Fellowes challenge. *Journalism Quarterly*, 68, pp. 823–828.

Ruggiero, G. (1999). *Microradio and democracy: (Low) power to the people*. New York: Seven Stories Press.

Sakolsky, R., & Dunifer, S. (eds.). (1998). *Seizing the airwaves: A free radio handbook*. San Francisco: AK Press.

Schiller, H. I. (1989). *Culture, inc.: The corporate takeover of public expression*. New York: Oxford University Press.

Shoemaker, P. J., & Reese, S. D. (1991). *Mediating the message: Theories and influences on mass media content.* New York: Longman.

Slattery, K. L., Hakanen, E. A., & Doremus, M. E. (1996). The expression of localism: Local TV news coverage in the new video marketplace. *Journal of Broadcasting and Electronic Media*, 40(3), pp. 403–413.

Soley, L. (1999). *Free radio: Electronic civil disobedience.* Boulder, CO: Westview Press.

Stavitsky, A. G. (1994). The changing conception of localism in U.S. public radio. *Journal of Broadcasting and Electronic Media*, 38(1), pp. 19–33.

Stavitsky, A. G., Avery, R. K., & Vanhala, H. (2001). From class d to LPFM: The high-powered politics of low-powered radio. *Journalism and Mass Communication Quarterly*, 78(2), pp. 340–355.

Streeter, T. (1996). *Selling the air: A critique of the policy of commercial broadcasting in the United States.* Chicago: University of Chicago Press.

Taylor, P. (1998, October). Pirate radio fights for legitimacy, pirates claim they bring diversity to the airwaves, FCC vs. Low-watt radio: does limited spectrum justify limited free speech? Outlaws of the airwaves: pirate radio prepares to walk the plank for the first amendment (3 part series), Free Speech: The Freedom Forum On-line at www.freedomforum.org/speech/.

Touraine, A. (1981). *The voice and the eye: An analysis of social movements.* Cambridge: Cambridge University Press.

Tristani, G. (1998, May 21). Broadcast views. Speech given to the Federal Communications Bar Association. Available on-line at www.fcc.gov/Speeches/Tristani/spgt808.html.

U.S. v. Any and All Radio Station Transmission Equipment. (1997). 976 F.Supp. 1255 (D. Minn. 1997).

U.S. V. Any and All Radio Station Transmission Equipment, located at 2903 Bent Oak Highway, Adrian Michigan (1998). 97-CV-73527 (Mich. Dist. Ct. August 7, 1998).

U.S. v. Dunifer. (1998a). 997 F. Supp. 1235 (N.D. Cal.).

———. (1998b, August 7). No. C-94-03542 CW. Motion to Alter. Available on-line at www.radio4all.org/news/frb-motiontoamend.html.

———. (1997, November 12). No. C-94-03542 CW. Order denying plaintiff's motion for summary judgment without prejudice and requesting further briefing. Available on-line at www.368Hayes.com/111297decision.html.

———. (1995, January 30). No. C-94-03542 CW. Memorandum and order denying plaintiff's motion for preliminary injunction and staying this action. Available on-line at www.368Hayes.com/microradio.opposition.pi.html.

———. (1994, December 2). No. C-94-03542 CW. Defendant's motion in opposition to plaintiff's motion for preliminary injunction. Available on-line at www.368Hayes.com/microradio.opposition.pi.html.

———. (1994, October 6). No. C-94-03542 CW.

U.S. Federal Communication Commission v. Prayze FM a/k/a Incom, L.L.C. and Mark Blake. (1998, September 11). 3.98-CV-00529 (Conn. Dist. Ct. September 11, 1998).

U.S. House Commerce Committee, U.S. House of Representatives. (2000, February 17). FCC's spectrum management responsibilities hearing.

Walker, J. (1998, March 9). Rebel radio: The FCC's absurd new crusade (against low-power "pirate" broadcasters), *The New Republic*, p. 11.

———. (1997, August 1). With friends like these: Why community radio does not need the corporation for public broadcasting. Cato Institute Policy Analysis. Available on-line at www.cato.org/pubs.

Warner, E. (1996). *Inside the FCC: A comprehensive profile of the U.S. federal communi-
    cations commission.* Alexandria, VA: Telecom Publishing Group.
www.radio4all.org. (1998). A micro radio information clearinghouse on the Internet.
Zald, M., & McCarthy, J. (1987). *Social movements in an organizational society.* New
    Brunswick, NJ: Transaction.

Index

About the Author

ANDY OPEL is an Assistant Professor in the Department of Communication at Florida State University, where he teaches documentary video production and critical media studies. He is the co-editor of *Representing Resistance: Media, Civil Disobedience, and the Global Justice Movement* (Praeger, 2003). His work has appeared in *Enviropop: Studies in Enviromental Rhetoric and Popular Culture* and the *Journal of American Culture*. His research interests include the emerging media and democracy movement as well as the intersection of consumer culture and the environment.